Listening *to the* Qur'ān

Listening *to the* Qur'ān

INSIGHTS, COMMANDS AND GUIDANCE FOR OUR LIFE

KHALID BAIG

openmind press
Garden Grove • California

Openmind Press, Garden Grove, CA 92842

First edition Rabīʿ al-Awwal 1435 / January 2014

Printed in the United States of America

23 22 21 20 19 18 17 16 15 14 1 2 3 4

ISBN 978-0-9755157-4-7

Library of Congress Control Number: 2013922750

∞ The paper used in this publication meets the minimum requirements of the American National Standard for Information Sciences - Permanence of Paper for Printed Materials, ANSI Z39.48-1984.

www.openmindpress.com

كِتَٰبٌ أَنزَلْنَٰهُ إِلَيْكَ مُبَٰرَكٌ لِّيَدَّبَّرُوٓا۟ ءَايَٰتِهِۦ وَلِيَتَذَكَّرَ أُو۟لُوا۟
ٱلْأَلْبَٰبِ ﴿٢٩﴾

(Here is) a Book which We have sent down unto you, full of blessings, that they may ponder over its āyahs, and that those who are endowed with insight may take them to heart. (Sād 38:29)

قَدْ جَآءَكُم مِّنَ ٱللَّهِ نُورٌ وَكِتَٰبٌ مُّبِينٌ ﴿١٥﴾ يَهْدِى
بِهِ ٱللَّهُ مَنِ ٱتَّبَعَ رِضْوَٰنَهُۥ سُبُلَ ٱلسَّلَٰمِ وَيُخْرِجُهُم
مِّنَ ٱلظُّلُمَٰتِ إِلَى ٱلنُّورِ بِإِذْنِهِۦ وَيَهْدِيهِمْ إِلَىٰ صِرَٰطٍ
مُّسْتَقِيمٍ ﴿١٦﴾

There has come to you from Allāh a light, and a Book Manifest. Whereby Allāh guides whosoever follows His good pleasure in the ways of peace and brings them forth from the depths of darkness into the light by His leave; and He guides them to a straight path. (Al-Mā'idah 5:15-16)

Transliteration Key

ء (ىٔإأ)	’ (a slight catch in the breath)	غ	gh (similar to French r)
ا	a	ف	f
ب	b	ق	q (heavy k, from the throat)
ة and ت	t (ة has an “h” sound at the end of a sentence)	ك	k
ث	th (as in “thorn”)	ل	l
ج	j	م	m
ح	ḥ (heavy h, from deep within the throat)	ن	n
خ	kh (“ch” in Scottish loch)	ه	h (as in “help”)
د	d (the hard “th” in “the”)	و	w
ذ	dh (the soft “th” in “the”)	ي	y (as in “yellow”)
ر	r		**Vowels**
ز	z	ـَ ـً	a (slightly softer than the “u” in “but”); an
س	s	ـِ ـٍ	i (as in “in”); in
ش	sh	ـُ ـٌ	u (“oo” in “book”); un
ص	ṣ (heavy s, from the upper mouth)	آ ا ٰ	ā (elongated a, as when you would stretch the “a” in “plastic”)
ض	ḍ (heavy d, from the upper mouth)	آ	ā at the start of a word, ’ā in the middle (pronounced like اَءَ)
ط	ṭ (heavy t, from the upper mouth)	و and ٗ	ū (“u” in “glue”)
ظ	ẓ (heavy z, from the upper mouth)	ي and ٖ	ī (“ee” in “feet”)
ع	‘ (like two a’s from deep within the throat)	ـّ	stress symbol, indicated by repetition of letter

Honorifics

سُبْحَانَهُ وَتَعَالَى	Glorified and Most High	ﷺ	May Allāh’s blessings and peace be upon him
عَلَيْهِ السَّلَام	May peace be upon him	رَضِيَ اللهُ عَنْهَا , رَضِيَ اللهُ عَنْهُ	May Allāh be pleased with him/her

Contents

Juz Twelve 85

Juz Thirteen 91

Juz Fourteen 101

Juz Fifteen 109

بسم الله الرحمن الرحيم

Introduction

This book grew from the daily *tarāwīḥ* reflections I wrote during Ramadan 1434. Tarāwīḥ is a unique phenomenon. While other religions claim to possess the Word of God, there is none that can show a book that commands anything even remotely comparable to the devotion that the Qur'ān commands and has commanded all through the centuries. Where else can you find millions of people all around the world standing in long prayers for a whole month to listen to an entire book being recited from memory?

However while our devotion to the Words of Allāh is unsurpassed, our devotion to the Message of Allāh requires more. We need to understand and reflect on the wisdom and commands contained in the Divine Words so that we are truly listening to them and not just hearing them. That is the basic idea behind this effort. I selected a few āyahs from every night's recitation to reflect on their message as it relates to our life and our challenges today. This was published on www.albalagh.net and distributed to a small email list. The feedback I received encouraged me to compile these in this book form. For this purpose these were much expanded and thoroughly revised and edited. In some cases I have also used passages from my first book, *First Things First*. Each of the thirty sections in this book consists of selected āyahs from the corresponding *juz* of the Qur'ān.

This is not meant to replace any commentary or *tafsīr*. It is only meant to start us thinking about some important Qur'ānic messages thereby making the listening more rewarding, more enriching, and more beneficial for our individual and collective lives. Such reflection is important for developing a strong personal relationship with the Qur'ān. The Qur'ān demands it by asking, "Will they not, then, ponder over this Qur'ān? – or are there locks upon their hearts?" (Muḥammad 47:24).

Obviously not everyone will become a Qur'ān scholar but every Muslim must develop a personal relationship with the Qur'ān. This requires regularly reading and reflecting. It is hoped that this short collection of reflections and observations will stimulate us to do that. Of course the exercise may whet our appetite for a more detailed study for which a number of translations and commentaries are available. But even then we should not forget that our purpose is to listen to the Qur'ān itself; the external aids are just meant to help in that goal.

The Qur'ānic translations in this book have been chosen carefully from the works of Mufti Taqi Usmani, Abdullah Yūsuf Ali, Marmaduke Pickthal, Muḥammad Asad, and Arthur J. Arberry.

In this work I was helped by my daughter Sumayya and my son Muneeb, both of whom graduated from madrasas in Pakistan in addition to receiving schooling in the US. Sumayya helped with searching the Arabic source texts, especially Hadith collections and commentaries. Both of them helped with proofreading, editing of the text, and typesetting. This has become a better book as a result of their hard work and constructive suggestions.

If you find any good in this book, please pray for me and those who helped in its production. If you find any errors, please inform me so they can be corrected.

May Allāh accept this effort and make this book a means of strengthening our relationship with the Qur'ān.

Khalid Baig
Muḥarram 1435
December 2013

Juz One

Taʿwwudh

أَعُوْذُ بِاللهِ مِنَ الشَّيْطَانِ الرَّجِيْم

I seek protection from Allāh against the accursed Satan.

We always begin our recitation of the Qur'ān by saying these words. This is not an āyah of the Qur'ān but the Qur'ān commanded us to seek this protection in the following āyah:

فَإِذَا قَرَأْتَ ٱلْقُرْءَانَ فَٱسْتَعِذْ بِٱللَّهِ مِنَ ٱلشَّيْطَٰنِ ٱلرَّجِيمِ ﴿٩٨﴾

Now whenever you read this Qur'ān, seek refuge with Allāh from Satan, the accursed. (An-Naḥl 16:98)

The first step in any successful communication is to make sure the communication link is solid and all external interference is eliminated. In receiving the communication from on High, the external interference that we have to be most concerned with is that of the whisperings and persuasions of our hidden enemy—the Satan.

As the next āyah in Sūrah an-Naḥl makes clear, the way to protect ourselves from satanic influences is by entrusting our affairs to Allāh. ("He (Satan) is such that he has no authority over those who believe and place trust in their Lord," An-Naḥl 16:99) It is those who rely on their own powers, physical as well as intellectual, who become easy prey to the machinations of the Satan.

Anyone who begins his interaction with the Qur'ān by seeking Allāh's help has put himself in the right state of mind for benefiting from Allāh's Words—provided this is a conscious and sincere act. He has established a secure communication link so he can begin to listen to the Words of Allāh as he reads or hears them.

Bismillāh

بِسْمِ ٱللَّهِ ٱلرَّحْمَٰنِ ٱلرَّحِيمِ

In the name of Allāh the Most Beneficent, the Most Merciful.

We begin every significant act by invoking the name of Allāh and remembering His mercy and kindness. It is a measure of the extraordinary importance of the right beginning that the very first revelation began with this command: "Read in the name of your Sustainer."[1] It was not just a command to read—as expropriated later by those who would use it to provide Islamic sanction for secular pursuits—but a command to read in the name of Allāh. (See more on this in the reflections on the last juz).

Beginning in the name of Allāh helps filter out acts and intentions that are disapproved by Him. It makes us conscious that Allāh is watching so we do not take wrong

1 *Al-Qur'ān*, al-ʿAlaq 96:1.

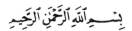

turns after starting. It assures us of Allāh's help in completing it successfully.

Pagans in Arabia, as elsewhere, used to begin any task in the name of their idols. In the secular "enlightened" West many a time people begin important projects by saying "knock on wood." This is how people ward off evils in the old and new worlds of superstition. In contrast a Muslim seeks guidance, help, and support from none other than Allāh—the Merciful Lord of the worlds. His day is filled with the calls of Bismillāh. It is Bismillāh before taking a shower, before putting on clothes, before eating, before getting on his ride, before starting his work, before starting a meeting, before signing an important paper, before taking a baby step, before taking a gigantic leap. And he can feel the blessings—the strength, the confidence, the peace of mind—this invocation brings throughout his days and nights.

Sūrah al-Fātiḥah

This sūrah is an extraordinary petition taught by the One to whom the petition is to be made. While ṣalāh is the most important act of worship in a Muslim's life, Sūrah al-Fātiḥah is the most important part of ṣalāh. It is recited in every rakʿah (unit) of every ṣalāh.

This sūrah deals with the fundamental questions of life. Where are we coming from? Where are we going? What is the purpose of life? These are the issues that humanity has been grappling with throughout its history. In seven short āyahs this sūrah answers these questions. This entire universe, and others that may be out there, are created by Allāh Most High, Who is the Sustainer of them all. He is the Benevolent and Merciful God. He alone deserves all the praise for all the goodness in the world and all thanks for all the blessings and favors that we have received and continue to receive throughout our lives. He is also the Master of the Day of Judgment when all the wrongs will be punished and right actions will be rewarded.

It follows then that our greatest concern should be to know right from wrong and have both the willingness and ability to follow the former and avoid the latter. This is the Straight Path that leads one straight to eternal success. The petition is that He shows us the Straight Path and makes it easy for us to follow it.

The Straight Path is not a theoretical construct. It is not defined by some nice principles or commandments which sound good as decoration pieces but cannot be put into practice. It refers to a road well travelled by real people who lived on this earth. They are referred to as blessed people here and fall into four categories as explained in an āyah in Sūrah al-Nisā': "Those who obey Allāh and the Messenger are with those whom Allāh has blessed, namely, the prophets, the Ṣiddīqīn (those who never deviated from the truth), the Shuhadā' (martyrs) and the righteous. And how goodly a company are these!"[2] Followers of the Straight Path have company. And what a great company it is!

Further, those who deviate from it are condemned in no uncertain terms as being either willful rejecters of Divine guidance or being careless about it. The point of this condemnation is to distance ourselves from them and their ways for our own protection.

While Sūrah al-Fātiḥah encapsulates the essence of ṣalāh, this āyah encapsulates the essence of al-Fātiḥah:

إِيَّاكَ نَعْبُدُ وَإِيَّاكَ نَسْتَعِينُ

You alone do we worship, and from You alone do we seek succor. (Al-Fātiḥah 1:4)

2 *Al-Qur'ān*, an-Nisā' 4:69.

This āyah is the affirmation of *tawḥīd* as both an article of faith as well as an overriding principle in total control of our actual life.

The word *ʿIbādah*, translated here as worship for lack of a better word, implies establishing an absolute master-slave relationship, which includes unquestioning obedience, total submission, and devotional acts like bowing and prostration. Pagans do worship idols by bowing and prostrating before them and treating them as gods. Others worship wealth, power, or celebrity in a figurative sense; they put them in the driver's seat in their life. This āyah is a bold and loud rejection of all of these acts of worship meant for anyone except Allāh. It is also a reminder that we should not start serving other gods even without realizing it.

The second part of this āyah is a corollary of the first part, but it needs an explanation. In our daily life we do offer and receive help from others. The Qur'ān itself mentions this help at many places. For example, it says: "Help each other in righteousness and piety, and do not help each other in sin and aggression."[3], thus regulating it by making righteousness or lack thereof as the basis for offering or withdrawing it. It praises the believers who help the Prophet ﷺ: "So, those who believe in him and support him, and help him and follow the light sent down with him,—those are the ones who are successful."[4] It reports that Prophet ʿĪsā (Jesus) عليه السلام asked his companions for help: "Who will be my helpers in Allāh's cause?"[5] Obviously this help is not negated here; it is offered and sought under the system of cause and effect, which itself has been created by Allāh for the normal running of this universe. What is negated ("We do not seek help from anyone except Allāh") is the help from other beings (e.g.

3 *Al-Qur'ān*, al-Mā'idah 5:2.
4 *Al-Qur'ān*, al-Aʿrāf 7:157.
5 *Al-Qur'ān*, Āl-i-ʿImrān 3:52.

saints and dead men) that is thought to transcend the system of cause and effect. Also negated is any help that is supposed to work independent of—or worse in defiance of—the Will of Allāh.

Allāh can help through means that we could not have imagined—even bypassing the system of cause and effect. And He also helps through the normal system of cause and effect. For every need we seek help from Him, and even when we call on other people for assistance we fully realize that they are not independent agents for providing that assistance.

Lastly we seek Allāh's help in performing the worship we promised in the first part. As a Ṣūfī master suggested, if one is finding it difficult to stay away from sins and to perform acts of worship, then reciting this āyah profusely will help greatly.

Guidance and its Prerequisites

ذَٰلِكَ ٱلْكِتَٰبُ لَا رَيْبَ ۛ فِيهِ ۛ هُدًى لِّلْمُتَّقِينَ ﴿٢﴾

That is the Book, wherein is no doubt, a guidance to the God-fearing. (Al-Baqarah 2:2)

We asked for guidance in Sūrah al-Fātiḥah. The response is immediate. The entire Qur'ān provides that guidance. It is here. Further, guidance requires certain knowledge. And this is the Book that contains certain knowledge and absolute truth. There is absolutely no room for doubt here. If someone entertains doubts about this Book, the problem is with them—not with the Book.

Right at the start we are being warned to shed our preconceived ways of discovering truth. With the proliferation and predominance of the secular and secularizing curriculum in the educational institutions throughout the world, this assumes even greater importance for us today. As Sayyid Naquib al-Attas writes: "(In rationalism) doubt is elevated as an epistemological method by means of which the rationalist and the secularist believe that truth is arrived at. But there is no proof that it is doubt and not something else other than doubt that enables one to arrive at truth. The arrival at truth is in reality the result of guidance, not of doubt."[6]

But there are prerequisites for benefitting from this guidance. These are mentioned here and in the next two āyahs. If we are sincere in seeking guidance, then we must also be serious in satisfying the prerequisites.

The first prerequisite is that the seeker must be a person of *taqwā* (translated here as "God-fearing"). If *taqwā* is the end result of guidance, how can it be its prerequisite? It is because *taqwā* is both an attitude and a state. The attitude is the prerequisite. The state is the result of a lifelong struggle. Ibn Abi 'd-Dunyā notes, "The beginning of taqwā is the right intention."[7] It is the intention to follow Allāh's command, to leave out whatever He forbids and carryout whatever He mandates. It is the intention to seek knowledge to translate it into action. It is a result of internalization of the knowledge that Allāh is the greatest so no one else can distract us from listening to Him and obeying Him. Only those with this attitude will be able to benefit from the guidance.

The resulting state was described by someone in a letter of advice to ᶜAbdullāh ibn az-Zubayr رضي الله عنه: "The people of taqwā are known by these signs: Patience in the face of hardships, contentment with the Will of Allāh, gratitude to

6 Sayyid Naquib al-Attas, *Prolegomena to the Metaphysics of Islam: An Exposition of the Fundamental Elements of the Worldview of Islam*, 117.

7 Ibn Abi 'd-Dunyā, as quoted in Jalāluddīn as-Suyūṭī, *Ad-Durr al-Manthūr fi t-Tafsīr bil Ma'thūr*, Sūrah al-Baqarah, verse 2, 1:58. [Dār Iḥyā t-Turāth al-ᶜArabī].

Allāh for all the good things in life and humble submission to His commands."[8]

ٱلَّذِينَ يُؤْمِنُونَ بِٱلْغَيْبِ وَيُقِيمُونَ ٱلصَّلَوٰةَ وَمِمَّا رَزَقْنَٰهُمْ يُنفِقُونَ ﴿٣﴾

Who believe in (the existence of and the knowledge given by Allāh about) that which is beyond the reach of human perception, and are constant in prayer, and spend on others out of what We provide for them as sustenance. (Al-Baqarah 2:3)

The visible spectrum is only a small fraction of the total reality. Everything beyond that is *al-ghayb*. While science, of necessity, deals only with the perceptible world, scientism insists that that is all there is to it. The successful guidance seeker is the one who is not blinded by this loud but false assertion. He is fully aware that the fundamental questions of life—about the existence of God and the purpose of creation, the life after death, the existence of spiritual forces, and so forth cannot be answered by science. He seeks them in revelation and finds them in the Qur'ān and its explanation in the Hadith.

Since seeking guidance is not just an academic exercise, the true seeker has these two other qualities that encompass practical application of the guidance in all areas of life. He is always ready to follow the guidance, whether the demands are made on his body (e.g. ṣalāh) or his possessions (e.g. spending in the path of Allāh).

وَٱلَّذِينَ يُؤْمِنُونَ بِمَآ أُنزِلَ إِلَيْكَ وَمَآ أُنزِلَ مِن قَبْلِكَ وَبِٱلْءَاخِرَةِ هُمْ يُوقِنُونَ ﴿٤﴾

And who believe in what has been revealed to you and what was revealed before you; and who are certain of the Hereafter. (Al-Baqarah 2:4)

8 ᶜAbdullāh ibn az-Zubayr as quoted in Ibid.

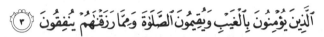

It is obvious that the Qur'ān will provide guidance to those who believe in it. But why the requirement of belief in the previous scriptures? It is so because we must believe in the historic continuity of the revealed guidance. The coming of Prophet Muḥammad ﷺ was not an historic anomaly but the culmination of a long chain of Prophets (124,000 in all according to a famous report), all of whom came with the same message.

This is a fundamental point in Islam's worldview. Humanity did not start its journey on this earth in the darkness of ignorance; it started it in full light of Divine guidance. By succumbing to temptations, human beings periodically deviated from that path and chose darkness over light. Spiritually and morally we have not been evolving, but rather deviating, and then being called back to the Straight Path by the Messengers of Allāh. We believe in them all, not to seek guidance from the previous scriptures or prophets (because according to the Divine plan they were not preserved), but to affirm our conviction about the system of guidance whose last manifestation is the coming of Prophet Muḥammad ﷺ.

With this worldview it is easy to see every new philosophy of life not as a mark of evolutionary progress but as another deviation, another failure, another move to darkness.

This āyah also implies the finality of Prophet Muḥammad ﷺ, since it does not mention any upcoming prophets. This is in contrast to āyah 3:81, which says that the followers of the previous prophets were told about the coming of Prophet Muḥammad ﷺ and asked to pledge that they would accept him as the Prophet and support him.

Congregational Prayer

وَأَقِيمُواْ ٱلصَّلَوٰةَ وَءَاتُواْ ٱلزَّكَوٰةَ وَٱرْكَعُواْ مَعَ ٱلرَّٰكِعِينَ ﴿٤٣﴾

And be steadfast in Ṣalāh (prayer), and pay Zakāh, and bow down with those who bow down. (Al-Baqarah 2:43)

The bowing mentioned here refers to the position in ṣalāh called *rukūʿ*. Of course what we are being required to do is to perform the entire ṣalāh, and not just rukūʿ, in congregation. This congregational ṣalāh is highly desirable; according to the majority of the jurists it is an emphasized sunnah. This applies to the five daily ṣalāhs and ṣalāh of Jumuʿah and ʿEīds, as they are all mandatory. It does not extend to the nafl ṣalāhs, which should be offered individually. Through this arrangement a balance is struck between public and private worship.

By extension we can also understand the balance between individual and collective rights and responsibilities prescribed by Islam. Our accountability before Allāh will be on an individual basis. But we live and worship in a community. Sūrah al-Fātiḥah, the essential part of every ṣalāh, uses the plural form; It is *we* not *I* seeking the Straight Path. It follows that we will be travelling on it together. The four pillars of Islam, ṣalāh, zakāh, fasting, and ḥajj are all collective acts. All were ordained (zakāh, fasting, and ḥajj) or given final shape (ṣalāh) in Madinah where Muslims could live in a community. Even when travelling, for whatever reason, we are asked to choose an *amīr* so the travel will be an organized one. Both the individual and the group are controlled by the Sharīʿah, which makes sure we avoid all excesses in their interaction.

The West has gone from the extremes of collectivism and totalitarianism to the extremes of individualism. It is important to remember that the middle course of Islam avoids both extremes.

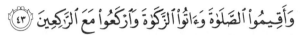

Juz Two

The Middle Nation

وَكَذَٰلِكَ جَعَلْنَـٰكُمْ أُمَّةً وَسَطًا لِّتَكُونُوا۟ شُهَدَآءَ عَلَى ٱلنَّاسِ وَيَكُونَ ٱلرَّسُولُ عَلَيْكُمْ شَهِيدًا

And thus have We willed you to be a community of the middle way, so that (with your lives) you might bear witness to the truth before all mankind, and that the Apostle might bear witness to it before you. (Al-Baqarah 2:143)

Ummatan Waṣaṭan can be translated as the middle nation, the best nation, and an Ummah justly balanced. The phrase captures the essence of Islam, which is to shun all excesses. At other places (e.g. Al-Mā'idah 5:12) the Qur'ān refers to the path it shows as *sawā as-sabīl*. Abdullah Yūsuf Ali explains: "The Arabic word sawā signifies smoothness as opposed to roughness; symmetry as opposed to want of plan; equality or proportion as opposed to want of design; rectitude as opposed to crookedness; a mean as opposed to extremes; and fitness for the object held in view as opposed to faultiness."

This āyah charters the Ummah to be a force against extremism. Extremism is a product of ignorance. Given two extreme points on a straight line, anyone can point out where the middle point lies. But a person who cannot see the entire line will also miss the middle point. He may be sitting on an extreme edge, yet congratulate himself for being in the middle.

Our own instruments of observation and intellect, wonderful as they are, are simply not up to the task of finding the perfectly balanced course in the complex, ever-changing, multidimensional maze, which is the real life. Yet we know that we do need to find it. Our physical well-being requires that we eat a well balanced diet and follow the course of moderation. Our economic, social, and spiritual well-being similarly demands finding the balanced approach and the moderate course in all these spheres. Our total well-being requires finding the path of moderation for our entire life.

Hence this charter. It says that the middle path is the one shown by the Messenger ﷺ to us so we can show it to the rest of humanity. Paths that deviate from it deviate toward extremism of one form or another—even though they may be slickly packaged as being paths of moderation.

The Prophet's Role, Our Responsibilities

كَمَآ أَرۡسَلۡنَا فِيكُمۡ رَسُولٗا مِّنكُمۡ يَتۡلُواْ عَلَيۡكُمۡ ءَايَٰتِنَا
وَيُزَكِّيكُمۡ وَيُعَلِّمُكُمُ ٱلۡكِتَٰبَ وَٱلۡحِكۡمَةَ وَيُعَلِّمُكُم مَّا لَمۡ
تَكُونُواْ تَعۡلَمُونَ ١٥١

As also We have sent in your midst a messenger from among you, who recites to you Our revelations, and purifies you, and teaches you the Book and the wisdom, and teaches you what you did not know. (Al-Baqarah, 2:151)

See the repeated reference to "you." This āyah describes the assignments of the Prophet ﷺ regarding *us*. That automatically fixes our responsibilities regarding each one of these tasks. It was his job to teach; it remains our job to learn. It is our job to learn the recitation of the Qur'ān as he taught, to get purified, to learn the Book and wisdom, and learn whatever he came to teach us. For each discipline, there are unbroken chains of teachers going back to the Prophet ﷺ from whom we can learn. The Qur'ān teachers, sufi masters, scholars, Hadith experts, and jurists are all there as are the books they have produced for our education.

This message is repeated in An-Nisā' 3:164 where it begins by saying that "Allāh has surely conferred favor on the believers" by sending the Messenger ﷺ with these tasks. We need to ask ourselves whether we are showing gratefulness for this favor.

When Calamity Strikes

ٱلَّذِينَ إِذَآ أَصَٰبَتۡهُم مُّصِيبَةٞ قَالُوٓاْ إِنَّا لِلَّهِ وَإِنَّآ إِلَيۡهِ رَٰجِعُونَ ١٥٦

Who, when a suffering visits them, say, "Verily, unto Allāh do we belong and, verily, unto Him we shall return." (Al-Baqarah, 2:156)

While most of us may know these words and use them at the death of someone, their true significance escapes many. The preceding and subsequent āyahs give glad tidings to those who say these words at the time of any calamity declaring, "Those are the ones upon whom there are blessings from their Lord, and mercy as well; and those are the ones who are on the right path."[1] According to a hadith these blessed words are a special gift of Allāh for this Ummah. That is why we do not find even previous prophets using them.

1 *Al-Qur'ān*, al-Baqarah, 2:157.

Their use should not be limited to the occasion of death. According to a hadith, everything that hurts a believer is the suffering mentioned here. Every instance of discomfort is an occasion for saying these words and getting the reward for being patient. The Prophet ﷺ showed by example that the scope of usage of these words extends to small things as well: a thorn prick, an insect bite, a lamp running out of oil, a shoe lace breaking.

Finally we must say these words with full consciousness that everything indeed belongs to Allāh and must return to Him. When we lose a person or a thing, they have simply gone back to the One to whom they belonged. This consciousness will help us face any loss with dignity.

True Piety

لَّيْسَ ٱلْبِرَّ أَن تُوَلُّوا۟ وُجُوهَكُمْ قِبَلَ ٱلْمَشْرِقِ وَٱلْمَغْرِبِ وَلَٰكِنَّ ٱلْبِرَّ مَنْ ءَامَنَ
بِٱللَّهِ وَٱلْيَوْمِ ٱلْءَاخِرِ وَٱلْمَلَٰٓئِكَةِ وَٱلْكِتَٰبِ وَٱلنَّبِيِّۦنَ وَءَاتَى ٱلْمَالَ عَلَىٰ
حُبِّهِۦ ذَوِى ٱلْقُرْبَىٰ وَٱلْيَتَٰمَىٰ وَٱلْمَسَٰكِينَ وَٱبْنَ ٱلسَّبِيلِ وَٱلسَّآئِلِينَ
وَفِى ٱلرِّقَابِ وَأَقَامَ ٱلصَّلَوٰةَ وَءَاتَى ٱلزَّكَوٰةَ وَٱلْمُوفُونَ بِعَهْدِهِمْ
إِذَا عَٰهَدُوا۟ ۖ وَٱلصَّٰبِرِينَ فِى ٱلْبَأْسَآءِ وَٱلضَّرَّآءِ وَحِينَ ٱلْبَأْسِ ۗ أُو۟لَٰٓئِكَ ٱلَّذِينَ
صَدَقُوا۟ ۖ وَأُو۟لَٰٓئِكَ هُمُ ٱلْمُتَّقُونَ ﴿١٧٧﴾

True piety does not consist merely in turning your faces towards the east or the west—but truly pious is he who believes in Allāh and the Last Day and the angels and the Book and the Prophets, and gives wealth, despite (his) love for it, to relatives, orphans, the helpless, the wayfarer, and to those who ask, and for the freeing of human beings from bondage and observes the Ṣalāh (prayers) and pays Zakāh; and (truly pious are) they who keep their promises whenever they make a promise, and are patient in misfortune and hardship and in time of peril. Such are the people of truth, the Allāh-fearing." (Al-Baqarah, 2:177)

Turning our face toward the Kaʿbah is a requirement in offering ṣalāh. Earlier āyahs in this sūrah detailed the commandments regarding this requirement. Here the issue is being put in proper perspective. The external forms of the prescribed acts of worship are important, but they should not distract us from focusing on the essence of piety which is described here. While paying attention to the external forms of worship, we should never lose sight of the attributes in this āyah. Other people have gone to two extremes in this matter. Some discarded the forms altogether. Others gave them so much weight, they lost the essence. The middle path of Islam requires that we avoid both extremes.

Spouses: The Metaphor of Garments

هُنَّ لِبَاسٌ لَّكُمْ وَأَنتُمْ لِبَاسٌ لَّهُنَّ

They are (like) a garment for you and you are (like) a garment for them. (Al-Baqarah 2:187)

The first thing this āyah tells us is that both husbands and wives equally need each other. Each one needs the other just as they need their garments. Realizing this mutual dependency will mold attitudes which are exactly opposite of the attitudes generated by a notion of independence, which is so prevalent today and has been so disastrous.

Further, the metaphor of garment defines the nature of relationship between spouses. It implies intimacy, comfort, covering, and protection. Our garments provide physical protection from the elements; the protection spouses provide is also spiritual and moral. The ideal husband and wife will help protect each other from sins.

Wine and Gambling

يَسْـَٔلُونَكَ عَنِ ٱلْخَمْرِ وَٱلْمَيْسِرِ ۖ قُلْ فِيهِمَآ إِثْمٌ كَبِيرٌ وَمَنَٰفِعُ لِلنَّاسِ وَإِثْمُهُمَآ أَكْبَرُ مِن نَّفْعِهِمَا

They ask you about intoxicants and gambling. Say, "In both there is great sin, and some benefit for people. But the evil which they cause is greater than the benefit which they bring." (Al-Baqarah, 2:219)

It is one of the Prophet's ﷺ great miracles that he made an entire people kick their deeply rooted drinking habit in a short period of time. He turned the Arabian Peninsula and subsequently every Muslim land into a dry land.

This is one of the earlier āyahs that started this unprecedented revolution. It just declared that the harms of wine far outweighed its benefits, without any discussion of its legal ruling. Then, the āyah that prohibited drinking around the time of the five daily ṣalāhs was revealed.[2] Finally, a total prohibition of wine was declared.[3]

The Qur'ānic messages were amplified by the Prophetic statements and actions. He said: "Allāh has cursed wine, its drinker, its server, its seller, its buyer, its presser, the one for whom it is pressed, the one who carries it, and the one to whom it is carried."[4]

When a total prohibition was proclaimed the Prophet ﷺ said: "Verily Allāh, the Exalted, has forbidden wine. So who hears this verse and he has anything of it with him, he should

2 *Al-Qur'ān*, an-Nisā', 4:43.

3 *Al-Qur'ān*, al-Mā'idah, 5:90–91.

4 Ibn 'Umar ؓ in *Sunan Abū Dāwūd*, كتاب الأشربة, [Book: Drinks], no. 3674.

neither drink it nor sell it."[5] And this hadith goes on to report that after this, "The people then brought whatever they had of it with them and spilled it on the streets of Madinah."

The miraculous eradication of drinking with all its evils demands reflection. How was it done? This is how: Minds were prepared, commands were issued for restricting and then totally prohibiting all use of and trade in alcohol, and punishments were declared and strictly enforced for violators. It was all based on *īmān*, firm faith in Allāh and His promise of rewards and punishments, and sincere submission to His commands. The overwhelming majority stopped drinking upon hearing the command. A few people failed to do so and were brought into line through strict enforcement of Sharīʿah punishments. Education and enforcement is the winning mix of strategies for the eradication of all social evils. Today social evils proliferate because both are absent.

Rights of Women

وَلَهُنَّ مِثْلُ ٱلَّذِى عَلَيْهِنَّ بِٱلْمَعْرُوفِ ۚ وَلِلرِّجَالِ عَلَيْهِنَّ دَرَجَةٌ ۗ وَٱللَّهُ عَزِيزٌ حَكِيمٌ

And women shall have rights, similar to the rights against them, according to what is equitable. But men have a degree (of advantage) over them. And Allāh is Exalted in Power, Wise. (Al-Baqarah, 2:228)

This is the foundation over which the entire structure of spousal relations is built by Islam. In one word that basis is equity, not equality.

There are societies today that for centuries refused to consider women as human beings or to give them any rights. Now they have gone to one extreme from the other. Islam

5 Abū Saʿīd al-Khudrī ﷺ in *Ṣaḥīḥ Muslim*, باب تحريم بيع الخمر [Chapter: Prohibition of sale of wine].

has nothing to do with such extremism. When women had no rights in the world, it made the above declaration. That remains its Command today and forever. Similar rights, not same rights. Equity, not a blind equality. Both men and women are equal in their humanity, in their accountability before Allāh, in their responsibility to perform their assigned tasks and be judged based on their performance. But their assigned tasks are not the same. They have been given different capabilities by their Creator and their tasks are based on those capabilities. This differentiation is not an error that needs to be corrected. It is the only basis for building a healthy and prosperous society. Islam liberates a woman from the modern tyranny of having to become a man in order to have a sense of self worth and achievement.

If Muslims had done their job, they would be asking for universal rights for women as given by Islam and generally ignored in the world today. Based on our dismal performance, and the current discourse on the subject, that would be quite a revolutionary—and liberating—act. Islam's universal declaration of women's rights would include the following:

1. Men and women have been given dignity by their Creator, but forces of immorality and darkness attack it in many ways. A prevalent form of this attack on women is pornography. Pornography is an affront to the respect and honor of women and produces an atmosphere where other crimes against them become possible. In many countries it has become an "industry" and they are exporting this filth to all parts of the world. Newer technologies, especially the Internet have become mediums of choice for the purveyors of filth, posing a serious threat to morality everywhere. Pornography must be condemned and all trade in porn banned universally in the same way that dangerous drugs are banned.

2. Prostitution must be recognized as a despicable act of exploitation of women. No one who condones it can be taken seriously in their claims to respect women's rights.

3. It is the responsibility of the husband to provide for the family. Islam has freed the woman from this responsibility so she can take care of the home. All efforts to snatch this freedom and economic security from the women and forcing them out of the home into the labor force must be resisted.

4. Homemaking is a very honorable job and a serious responsibility; it is the foundation on which healthy societies can be built. The societies that disrespect homemaking lose the homemakers and end up with broken homes as can easily be witnessed in many parts of the world. It should be recognized that the trend to belittle the task of homemaking is anti-family and anti-society and must be curbed.

5. It is a Muslim woman's right to dress modestly, wear hijab, and refuse to be put on display. This right must be accepted universally and any effort to restrict this right must be recognized for what it is: religious discrimination and/or persecution.

6. There is only one legitimate form of the family, that created by the union between a man and woman as provided in all revealed religions. Any other form is not only immoral; it poses a serious threat to humanity.

7. Families should be protected from outside intrusion, especially intrusion by governments as much as possible. This also includes intrusion in the name of help. For resolution of family disputes, Islam suggests a three phase procedure.

A) Resolve the conflict within the home.
B) Resolve it within the family by involving elders from the families of husband and wife.
C) As a last resort resolve it through courts of law.

Generosity in Dealings

وَلَا تَنسَوُا الْفَضْلَ بَيْنَكُمْ

And do not forget magnanimity towards one another. (Al-Baqarah 2:237)

If we listened to this teaching, it would bring out a revolutionary change in our family and social relations. Healthy relationships require a healthy dose of generosity. When giving to others, we should be willing to give more than their due. When receiving, we should be willing to take less.

It is also significant that this has been mentioned during a discussion of divorce when anger and resentment would be at a high level. If a person can be generous even at that time, they can certainly be expected to be generous at other occasions. In that environment difficulties would be resolved amicably. If a people have that attitude, divorce would be uncommon among them, and a bitter divorce would be unheard of.

Today divorce attorneys work on an exactly opposite platform. They say, forget generosity. Get as much as you can from the other person. The more money you get the happier you would be. This false promise has filled the most affluent societies with walking wounded, people who appear to be doing fine, but are living with deep wounds in their souls. Unfortunately Muslims are also following in their footsteps, and are reaping the bitter harvest of broken homes and ruined lives.

Juz Three

Real Charity

ٱلَّذِينَ يُنفِقُونَ أَمْوَٰلَهُمْ فِى سَبِيلِ ٱللَّهِ ثُمَّ لَا يُتْبِعُونَ مَآ أَنفَقُوا۟ مَنًّا وَلَآ أَذًى ۙ لَّهُمْ أَجْرُهُمْ عِندَ رَبِّهِمْ وَلَا خَوْفٌ عَلَيْهِمْ وَلَا هُمْ يَحْزَنُونَ ﴿٢٦٢﴾

They who spend their wealth for the sake of Allāh and do not thereafter mar their spending by stressing their own benevolence and hurting (the feelings of the needy) shall have their reward with their Sustainer, and no fear need they have, and neither shall they grieve. (Al-Baqarah, 2:262)

Here is the definition of real charity in Islam; it must be given solely for the sake of Allāh.

It is easy to find the rich in all societies engaged in works of charity. They may do it to feel good, to advertise their generosity, to show their superiority over the receivers of their help, or just enjoy the praise it will bring. What is difficult is to give in charity to please Allāh alone without any of these incentives. The success of charitable fundraising methods that employ these incentives is sufficient proof of this fact.

The Qur'ān is emphatic that such tainted charity will bring not reward but punishment in the Hereafter. It is a matter of great concern that despite that, such methods are finding widespread use in the Muslim community.

Concern for Hearts Swerving

رَبَّنَا لَا تُزِغْ قُلُوبَنَا بَعْدَ إِذْ هَدَيْتَنَا وَهَبْ لَنَا مِن لَّدُنكَ رَحْمَةً ۚ إِنَّكَ أَنتَ الْوَهَّابُ ﴿٨﴾

O our Sustainer! Let not our hearts swerve from the Truth after You have guided us; and bestow upon us the gift of Your grace. Surely, You, and You alone, are the Grantor of bounties in abundance. (Āli ʿImrān, 3:8)

As the previous āyah states, this is the dua of those who are firmly grounded in knowledge. They never become complacent with their īmān (faith), as they are fully aware that one's īmān is one's most precious treasure and needs to be carefully guarded. Further they know they cannot guarantee its protection themselves as their hearts can come under the influence of Satan or their own inclinations towards evil, so they must turn to Allāh to seek His help in doing so. Additionally they appeal to the gift of Allāh's mercy in seeking this help as it is not a payment for their deeds. They beg for it, claiming no entitlement. Needless to say, it is unimaginable that anyone consciously making this duʿā will knowingly engage in such enterprises as may pose danger to his imān.

Creation of Jesus عليه السلام

إِنَّ مَثَلَ عِيسَىٰ عِندَ ٱللَّهِ كَمَثَلِ ءَادَمَ ۖ خَلَقَهُۥ مِن تُرَابٍ ثُمَّ قَالَ لَهُۥ كُن
فَيَكُونُ ﴿٥٩﴾

Surely, the case of ʿĪsā (Jesus), in the sight of Allāh, is like the case of Adam. He created him from dust, then He said to him, "Be", and he came to be. (Āli ʿImrān, 3:59)

This is the simple truth about the creation of human beings in general as well as that of Prophet Jesus عليه السلام. Evolution scientists rejected the first and have gone to complex and convoluted theories as an alternate explanation. Christians rejected the second and have gone to complex and unfathomable explanations about trinity and divinity of Prophet Jesus عليه السلام. To each we must ask: Based on what evidence do you reject the obvious, simple and straightforward explanation given here? Have you unearthed any facts—hard facts, not conjectures—that would show the impossibility of the assertion made here?

The Interfaith Dialogue

قُلْ يَٰٓأَهْلَ ٱلْكِتَٰبِ تَعَالَوْا۟ إِلَىٰ كَلِمَةٍ سَوَآءٍۭ بَيْنَنَا وَبَيْنَكُمْ أَلَّا نَعْبُدَ
إِلَّا ٱللَّهَ وَلَا نُشْرِكَ بِهِۦ شَيْـًٔا وَلَا يَتَّخِذَ بَعْضُنَا بَعْضًا أَرْبَابًا مِّن دُونِ
ٱللَّهِ ۚ فَإِن تَوَلَّوْا۟ فَقُولُوا۟ ٱشْهَدُوا۟ بِأَنَّا مُسْلِمُونَ ﴿٦٤﴾

Say, "O people of the Book, come to a word common between us and between you, that we worship none but Allāh, that we associate nothing with Him and that we shall not take human beings for our lords beside Allāh." Then, should they turn back, say, "Bear witness that we are Muslims." (Āli ʿImrān, 3:64)

This sets both the basis and the tone of the interfaith dialogue that Islam called for fourteen centuries ago. It is good that some Christians and Jews are showing active interest in interfaith dialogue today. Muslims must take part in it while making sure it remains within the parameters established here.

Juz Four

Muslim Unity

وَٱعْتَصِمُوا۟ بِحَبْلِ ٱللَّهِ جَمِيعًا وَلَا تَفَرَّقُوا۟ ۚ وَٱذْكُرُوا۟ نِعْمَتَ ٱللَّهِ عَلَيْكُمْ
إِذْ كُنتُمْ أَعْدَآءً فَأَلَّفَ بَيْنَ قُلُوبِكُمْ فَأَصْبَحْتُم بِنِعْمَتِهِۦٓ إِخْوَٰنًا وَكُنتُمْ عَلَىٰ
شَفَا حُفْرَةٍ مِّنَ ٱلنَّارِ فَأَنقَذَكُم مِّنْهَا ۗ كَذَٰلِكَ يُبَيِّنُ ٱللَّهُ لَكُمْ ءَايَٰتِهِۦ لَعَلَّكُمْ
تَهْتَدُونَ ١٠٣

And hold fast, all together, unto the bond with Allāh, and do not draw apart from one another. And remember the blessings which Allāh has bestowed upon you: how, when you were enemies, He brought your hearts together, so that through His blessing you became brethren; and (how, when) you were on the brink of a fiery abyss, He saved you from it. This is how Allāh makes His signs clear to you, so that you may take the right path. (Āli ʿImrān, 3:103)

Unity is a subject discussed often in Muslim circles. The problems caused by its absence at every level, from small local communities to the worldwide ummah, are too vivid to be ignored. Unfortunately we talk about unity the way we talk about the weather; something that is happening to us. We take no responsibility for it and thus assure that the sorry state of disunity will continue.

This āyah should change that fatal attitude for it starts with two command verbs, a do and a don't. Do hold fast together unto the bond with Allāh and do not cause divisions among yourself. The word used is *ḥabl* or rope. The metaphor is that of a lifeline thrown at us by Allāh. If we hold on to it we will be saved. It will keep us together as well as we will all be pulled by the same rope. This lifeline can never break. But we can choose to not hold on to it. This is the fundamental reason for all the disunity today. If we choose to attain unity on any other basis (e.g. nationalism, democracy, or economic goals) we will fail as has been witnessed in so many cases in recent history alone. Ultimately all of these appeal to interests that will collide at some point or another.

The brotherhood that brought the tribes that had been at war with each other for centuries is mentioned as a blessing. Not only the Muhājirs of Makkah and Anṣārs of Madinah were brought together in an exemplary brotherhood, so were the tribes of Aws and Khazraj, the Madinan tribes whose last war lasted for 120 years and ended only a short time before the coming of the Prophet ﷺ to Madinah.

But this blessing came when the new Muslim society had been taking steps that qualified it for receiving it. From the moment the Prophet ﷺ set his foot in Madinah he took steps to nurture brotherhood. Among the first hadith reported from that period is the famous one: "Spread salam, feed others, pray (nafl tahajjud ṣalāh) when the people are asleep, and you will enter the Paradise with ease." Here interpersonal relations were put at the same level as acts of worship. Greeting everyone and not just those with whom we have good terms was emphasized. So was inviting people to break bread together. Such seemingly minor acts have big consequences in nurturing brotherly love and creating the environment which promotes unity and stifles the negative feelings that cause disunity. It is remarkable how the smallest things that can cause ill feelings were elaborated. For example it was prohibited that in the presence of a third person two people should start a whispering conversation among themselves. This would make him feel left out. Making fun of each other was strictly prohibited on moral grounds.

Today we ignore all of these commands. Backbiting, suspicions, and slander are common. We are driven by personal interests and egos while running Islamic organizations. Then we complain that unity is not *happening* to us. Things will change only when we take personal responsibility for it.

Charter of the Ummah: Enjoining Good

كُنتُمْ خَيْرَ أُمَّةٍ أُخْرِجَتْ لِلنَّاسِ تَأْمُرُونَ بِٱلْمَعْرُوفِ وَتَنْهَوْنَ عَنِ
ٱلْمُنكَرِ وَتُؤْمِنُونَ بِٱللَّهِ ۗ وَلَوْ ءَامَنَ أَهْلُ ٱلْكِتَٰبِ لَكَانَ خَيْرًا
لَّهُم ۚ مِّنْهُمُ ٱلْمُؤْمِنُونَ وَأَكْثَرُهُمُ ٱلْفَٰسِقُونَ ﴿١١٠﴾

You are the best 'Ummah ever raised for (the good of) mankind. You enjoin the doing of what is right and forbid the doing of what is wrong and you believe in Allāh. (Āli 'Imrān, 3:110)

Here, promoting good, truth, and justice and checking evil and injustice in the community and the world is declared as the defining mission for this ummah. This gives rise to that cherished (and much maligned in the secular world) institution of *amr-bil-ma'rūf*.

In *amr-bil-ma'rūf*, the community of believers has a built-in self-correcting mechanism. Consider cruise control in an automobile. Once turned on, it keeps monitoring the car speed and pulling it towards the set point. It does not mean absence of tendency to deviate from the desired speed, only an effective mechanism for monitoring and countering it. What cruise control does for car speed, *amr-bil-maʿrūf* does for the direction of the society.

This mechanism works at two levels. At one level it is the responsibility of every member of the society. When we see a wrong we should correct it. A very famous hadith declares it as an issue of faith. "Whoever amongst you sees an evil should change it with his hand. If he is unable to do that then with his tongue. If he is unable to do that, then with his heart, and that is the weakest level of Īmān."[1] So if a person does not even feel bad about an evil, he has no faith whatsoever. Similarly we are encouraged to promote good. One hadith promises that a person who persuades another one to do some good deed will get the same reward as the person he persuaded. At this level the responsibility of every member of the society is for his or her own sphere of influence: family, friends, colleagues, neighbors. When taken together these spheres would encompass the entire society.

At a higher level this is a specialized task. A full time job for a qualified group to always monitor the direction of the society and fight deviations at a collective level.

We must remember that the Islamic society is the only society with a declared mission of promoting good and forbidding evil. So this is also a unique institution that will not be looked at kindly by those who oppose this objective. Further, its definition of good and evil is not subject to the whims and desires of every generation or the perceived interests of a nation-state. They are permanent concepts as defined in its unalterable sources: Qur'ān and Sunnah. In a world of moral relativism these permanent values are the hope for the whole mankind. To keep these alive in the society we need the institution of *amr-bil-maʿrūf*.

1 Abū Saʿīd al-Khudrī ﵁ in *Ṣaḥīḥ Muslim*, كتاب الايمان [Chapter: Faith].

Anti-Islamic Propaganda

لَتُبْلَوُنَّ فِىٓ أَمْوَٰلِكُمْ وَأَنفُسِكُمْ وَلَتَسْمَعُنَّ مِنَ ٱلَّذِينَ
أُوتُوا۟ ٱلْكِتَٰبَ مِن قَبْلِكُمْ وَمِنَ ٱلَّذِينَ أَشْرَكُوٓا۟ أَذًى
كَثِيرًا ۚ وَإِن تَصْبِرُوا۟ وَتَتَّقُوا۟ فَإِنَّ ذَٰلِكَ مِنْ عَزْمِ ٱلْأُمُورِ ﴿١٨٦﴾

You shall certainly be tried and tested in your possessions and in your persons; and you shall certainly hear much that will grieve you from those who received the Book before you and from those who worship many gods. But if you persevere patiently, and guard against evil, then that will be a determining factor in all affairs. (Āli ʿImrān, 3:186)

Many of us get unnerved when the propaganda machine goes in the attack mode. While it is our job to respond to the allegations and portray the correct image, nevertheless it is not right to get panicky and start appeasing to "correct the image." A Muslim must not be intimidated by false propaganda, no matter how ferocious. The Qur'ān mentions as a quality of the believers who love Allāh and are loved by Him that they strive in His path "fearing not the blame of any blamer."[2] It assures us that the propaganda will continue as part of our test. But it will not harm us if we persevere.

Wisdom and Science Education

إِنَّ فِى خَلْقِ ٱلسَّمَٰوَٰتِ وَٱلْأَرْضِ وَٱخْتِلَٰفِ ٱلَّيْلِ وَٱلنَّهَارِ لَءَايَٰتٍ
لِّأُو۟لِى ٱلْأَلْبَٰبِ ﴿١٩٠﴾

Surely, in the creation of the heavens and the earth, and the alternation of night and day, there are indeed Signs for men of wisdom. (Āli ʿImrān, 3:190)

2 *Al-Qur'ān*, al-Maidah 5:54.

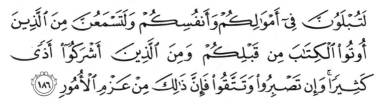

This āyah gives a totally revolutionary concept of wisdom. The truly wise person is one who looks at the universe and the phenomena taking place here, reflects on them, and sees the Hand of Allāh in all this. The observation of the creations leads him to the Creator. The more he reflects the more he remembers Allāh.

It follows that the person who remains disinterested or a disbeliever in the Creator while looking at the universe is not a person of understanding or wisdom. He may have the most prestigious degrees, yet he remains an ignorant person in reality.

This is the fundamental problem with the education of science today. It teaches that God is irrelevant to the running and study of the universe. This position itself is not scientific; it is not that science has discovered and proved that God is not there or is not running the universe. It is only a dogma that is forced on its students.

In schools throughout the Muslim world this dogma is being spread in the name of science education, with devastating results. That is why Islamization of the entire curriculum is so important.

Taqwā and Marital Bliss

يَٰٓأَيُّهَا ٱلنَّاسُ ٱتَّقُوا۟ رَبَّكُمُ ٱلَّذِى خَلَقَكُم مِّن نَّفْسٍ وَٰحِدَةٍ وَخَلَقَ مِنْهَا زَوْجَهَا وَبَثَّ
مِنْهُمَا رِجَالًا كَثِيرًا وَنِسَآءً ۚ وَٱتَّقُوا۟ ٱللَّهَ ٱلَّذِى تَسَآءَلُونَ بِهِۦ وَٱلْأَرْحَامَ ۚ إِنَّ ٱللَّهَ كَانَ
عَلَيْكُمْ رَقِيبًا ﴿١﴾

O Mankind! Have taqwā of your Sustainer, who has created you out of one living entity, and out of it created its mate, and out of the two spread abroad a multitude of men and women. And have taqwā of Allāh, in whose name you demand (your rights) from one another, and fear (the violation of the rights of) the ties of kinship. Surely, Allāh is watchful over you. (An-Nisā', 4:1)

This āyah should be familiar to anyone who has attended a Muslim wedding ceremony and listened to the khuṭbah of nikah. What is the relevance of this āyah to the marriage ceremony? Taqwā, as is usually imagined, involves visions of austere piety. In typical marriage ceremonies the atmosphere is as far away from any sense of taqwā as possible. Yet the short khuṭbah on this occasion heavily emphasizes taqwā.

While the atmosphere in these ceremonies is a great misfortune, the question remains: What does taqwā have to do with success in married life?

The short answer is, everything. Taqwā is the consciousness of Allāh and fear of displeasing Him. It applies to every aspect of our life, not just the acts of worship to which it is usually and erroneously restricted. And it is especially the taqwā in dealings which is the key to solving all marital problems. It is when problems arise—which is natural—that negative feelings of frustrations and anger are engendered, which lead to negative actions. Trouble starts in these moments of weakness. Taqwā in dealings—although not found easily even among otherwise religious people—is the key to maintaining a fair and balanced attitude exactly at these difficult times.

A husband or wife conscious of their accountability to Allāh will not get carried away in their anger nor will they be ready to exploit the weakness of the other party. They will be kind and patient. They will be willing to make sacrifices and compromises when indicated by the situation. They will be forgiving. They will not be preoccupied with their rights but with their responsibilities in marriage. The Prophetic guidance on this matter is sufficient to solve marital problems and bring about true marital bliss. Taqwā will make it possible for the couple to listen to the Prophetic advice even in the heat of the moment and benefit from it.

Juz Five

Fundamental Law of Business Dealings

يَـٰٓأَيُّهَا ٱلَّذِينَ ءَامَنُوا۟ لَا تَأْكُلُوٓا۟ أَمْوَٰلَكُم بَيْنَكُم بِٱلْبَـٰطِلِ
إِلَّآ أَن تَكُونَ تِجَـٰرَةً عَن تَرَاضٍ مِّنكُمْ

O you who believe, do not devour your wealth among yourselves by false means, unless it is trade conducted with your mutual consent. (An-Nisā', 4:29)

This is the fundamental law of Islam for all financial dealings. It declares all exploitation unlawful and stipulates two conditions for the acceptability of financial dealings. A) It should be a fair trade and B) it should be with free mutual consent. Trade includes sales, rentals, and employment of labor. It excludes interest transactions, since it is exchange of money for time and not for any valuable property. Deception and coercion also invalidate a transaction. All financial laws of Islam are governed by this fundamental law. Consent is so important that even charitable donations collected through pressure techniques are impermissible in Islam.

Today most marketing aims at precisely the opposite goals, whereby exaggerating the virtues and hiding the defects are considered acceptable marketing practices. Worse, creative marketing makes a virtue of such deceptions, equating successful exploitation with smartness. It is a travesty that business schools in the Muslim world today teach the same "sciences" and feel good about spreading "education."

Unhealthy Rivalry: Feminism and More

وَلَا تَتَمَنَّوْا۟ مَا فَضَّلَ ٱللَّهُ بِهِۦ بَعْضَكُمْ عَلَىٰ بَعْضٍ ۚ لِّلرِّجَالِ نَصِيبٌ
مِّمَّا ٱكْتَسَبُوا۟ ۖ وَلِلنِّسَآءِ نَصِيبٌ مِّمَّا ٱكْتَسَبْنَ ۚ وَسْـَٔلُوا۟ ٱللَّهَ مِن
فَضْلِهِۦٓ ۗ إِنَّ ٱللَّهَ كَانَ بِكُلِّ شَىْءٍ عَلِيمًا ﴿٣٢﴾

Do not covet something in which Allāh has made some of you superior to others. For men there is a share of what they earned, and for women, a share of what they earned. Pray to Allāh for His grace. Surely, Allāh is All-Aware of everything. (An-Nisā', 4:32)

This āyah was revealed in response to questions regarding disparity between men and women. Sayyidah Umm Salamah, the mother of believers رضي الله عنها, looking for an explanation, observed: "Men take part in battles and we do not. We do not take part in combat so we can become martyrs. Also our share in the inheritance is half theirs."[1] According to another report from ʿIkrimah some women said "We deeply desired that Allāh would let us participate in battles so we would get the same reward as men." According to another report a woman was concerned that since women have half the share in inheritance and are given half the weight as witnesses in

1 Umm Salamah رضي الله عنها in *Sunan at-Tirmidhī*, كتاب التفسير [Book: Tafsīr]; Umm Salamah رضي الله عنها in Al-Mustadrak ʿalaṣ-Ṣaḥīḥayn, باب تفسير سورة النساء [Section: Tafsīr of Sūrah an-Nisā'].

many cases, they would also get half the reward of men for all good deeds.

Lest anyone influenced by feminist ideology jump into confusion here, women were not seeking equal rank in the family or tribal hierarchy; they were rather concerned about rewards in the Hereafter. They wanted to make sure they would get equal wages of piety for equal piety. And they were assured, here as well as at many other places in the Qur'ān, that the rewards for good or bad deeds are the same for men and women.

While we are encouraged to compete with each other in performing good deeds, we should not get carried away with the idea of competition. Feminism is the result of taking competitiveness to extremes by seeking everything for women that applies to men. This is its foundation and this foundation is being demolished in no uncertain terms here.

If men are superior in some respects (like physical strength) so be it. That is Allāh's plan. If they are given the sole responsibility for earning a living for the family and therefore are given a bigger share in the inheritance in most circumstances, so be it. Their abilities are not the same. Their spheres are not the same. But within their sphere, ultimately everyone will get the rewards based on their own effort and ability. If they listen to this āyah, women will be content being women and will lead happy lives.

But the message is not to be limited to its immediate context. It is general and applies to all unhealthy rivalry. We have not been created equal in our appearance, skin color, physical strength, talents, and abilities. We should not waste any time comparing ourselves with others and lamenting our disadvantages in any of these things. We submit to the Will of Allāh in everything that is beyond our control. But we try to do the best in areas where we have been given freedom of action. And we seek Allāh's grace and mercy all the time.

Most of the psychological problems in the world would go away if we followed this one gem of advice.

Conflicts of Interest: Justice in the Face of Love

يَـٰٓأَيُّهَا ٱلَّذِينَ ءَامَنُوا۟ كُونُوا۟ قَوَّٰمِينَ بِٱلْقِسْطِ شُهَدَآءَ لِلَّهِ وَلَوْ عَلَىٰٓ
أَنفُسِكُمْ أَوِ ٱلْوَٰلِدَيْنِ وَٱلْأَقْرَبِينَ ۚ إِن يَكُنْ غَنِيًّا أَوْ فَقِيرًا فَٱللَّهُ أَوْلَىٰ
بِهِمَا ۖ فَلَا تَتَّبِعُوا۟ ٱلْهَوَىٰٓ أَن تَعْدِلُوا۟ ۚ وَإِن تَلْوُۥٓا۟ أَوْ تُعْرِضُوا۟ فَإِنَّ ٱللَّهَ كَانَ
بِمَا تَعْمَلُونَ خَبِيرًا ﴿١٣٥﴾

O you who believe! Stand out firmly for justice, as witnesses to Allāh, even as against yourselves, or your parents, or your kin, and whether it be (against) rich or poor: for Allāh can best protect both. Follow not the lusts (of your hearts), lest you swerve, and if you distort (the truth) or decline to do justice, verily Allāh is well-acquainted with all that you do. (An-Nisā' 4:135)

Under normal circumstances many people can be just. But Islam commands its followers to be just even in the face of strong conflicting emotions. In dealing with other human beings, two major impediments to justice are love and hatred. This āyah teaches us to overcome the first impediment when we are dealing with our closest relatives or even ourselves. Here is the resolution from the Qur'ān of the perennial conflict between self-interest and justice. Be just, even if it is against your narrowly defined self-interest or that of those very close to you.

Ignorant people think they are protecting their self-interest by being unjust to others. Their decision to be just or unjust may be based on a cold calculation of self-interest. But real faith in Allāh elevates one beyond that narrow-mindedness. This āyah reminds us that the real protector of interests of all people is Allāh and He will protect us when we follow His command to be just. The justice demanded by Islam permits no favoritism. The second impediment to justice is discussed in the next juz.

Juz Six

Basis for Cooperation

وَتَعَاوَنُوا۟ عَلَى ٱلْبِرِّ وَٱلتَّقْوَىٰ ۖ وَلَا تَعَاوَنُوا۟ عَلَى ٱلْإِثْمِ وَٱلْعُدْوَٰنِ

Help one another in furthering virtue and Allāh-consciousness, and do not help one another in furthering evil and aggression. (Al-Mā'idah, 5:2)

This is a fundamental principle that governs all our cooperation with others. Cooperative arrangements result from calculations that it will be, as normally phrased, a win-win situation. But what does that exactly mean? It means that both the parties entering into a pact of cooperation will achieve their self interest. However for Muslims, considerations of virtue override all other considerations. Any enterprise, no matter how attractive on the basis of self interest, is a no-no if it leads to sin, evil, or aggression.

Perfection of Religion

ٱلْيَوْمَ أَكْمَلْتُ لَكُمْ دِينَكُمْ وَأَتْمَمْتُ عَلَيْكُمْ نِعْمَتِى وَرَضِيتُ لَكُمُ
ٱلْإِسْلَٰمَ دِينًا

Today, I have perfected your religion for you, and have completed My blessing upon you, and chosen Islam as Dīn (religion and a way of life) for you. (Al-Mā'idah, 5:3)

This āyah was revealed at ʿArafāt in the afternoon of Friday, the 9th of Dhu 'l-Ḥijjah, 10 AH, eighty-one or eighty-two days before the death of the Prophet ﷺ. No legal injunction whatsoever was revealed after this. Here was the announcement that the sequence of revelations to the last of the prophets was now coming to an end. The deen, the system of beliefs and practices, was completed. It was perfected. People are free to acccpt or refuse to accept the message of the Qur'ān. But this categorical declaration does not leave any room for anyone to "improve" it or "reform" it.

Additionally this āyah contains the last legal ordinances ever revealed to the Prophet Muḥammad ﷺ. They deal with ḥalāl and ḥarām meat. This shows the importance of eating ḥalāl.

Conflict of Interest: Justice in the Face of Enmity

يَٰٓأَيُّهَا ٱلَّذِينَ ءَامَنُوا۟ كُونُوا۟ قَوَّٰمِينَ لِلَّهِ شُهَدَآءَ بِٱلْقِسْطِ ۖ وَلَا
يَجْرِمَنَّكُمْ شَنَـَٔانُ قَوْمٍ عَلَىٰٓ أَلَّا تَعْدِلُوا۟ ۚ ٱعْدِلُوا۟ هُوَ أَقْرَبُ
لِلتَّقْوَىٰ ۖ وَٱتَّقُوا۟ ٱللَّهَ ۚ إِنَّ ٱللَّهَ خَبِيرٌۢ بِمَا تَعْمَلُونَ ﴿٨﴾

O you who believe! Stand out firmly for Allāh, as witnesses to fair dealing, and let not the hatred of others to you make you swerve to wrong and depart from justice. Be just: that is next to Piety: and fear

Allāh. For Allāh is well-acquainted with all that you do. (Al-Mā'idah 5:8)

This āyah deals with the othcr equally potent impediment to justice: hatred. It commands loudly and clearly that you cannot do injustice even when you are dealing with the enemy.

The natural, uneducated, and uncivilized tendency is to treat the enemy as less than a human being; one who has no rights and deserves no justice or fairness. It was as true in the pre-Islamic tribal jahiliyyah (based on ignorance) society as it is today. See how Islam directly curbs it. It is a command to the believers, with a reminder that Allāh is watching you, that enmity of others cannot be used as an excuse for committing injustices against them.

Friendship with Enemies of Islam

يَٰٓأَيُّهَا ٱلَّذِينَ ءَامَنُوا۟ لَا تَتَّخِذُوا۟ ٱلَّذِينَ ٱتَّخَذُوا۟ دِينَكُمْ هُزُوًا وَلَعِبًا مِّنَ ٱلَّذِينَ أُوتُوا۟
ٱلْكِتَٰبَ مِن قَبْلِكُمْ وَٱلْكُفَّارَ أَوْلِيَآءَ ۚ وَٱتَّقُوا۟ ٱللَّهَ إِن كُنتُم مُّؤْمِنِينَ ﴿٥٧﴾

O you who have attained to faith! Do not take for your friends such as mock at your faith and make a jest of it—be they from among those who have been given the Book prior to you, or the disbelievers. But remain conscious of Allāh, if you are (truly) believers. (Al-Mā'idah, 5:57)

This āyah is self explanatory and sets the limits on interfaith friendship. Yūsuf Ali writes: "It is not right that we should be in intimate association with those to whom religion is either a subject of mockery or at best is nothing but a plaything. They may be amused, or they may have other motives for encouraging you. But your association with them will sap the earnestness of your Faith, and make you cynical and insincere."

Juz Seven

The Tyranny of Majority

قُل لَّا يَسْتَوِى ٱلْخَبِيثُ وَٱلطَّيِّبُ وَلَوْ أَعْجَبَكَ كَثْرَةُ ٱلْخَبِيثِ ۚ فَٱتَّقُوا۟ ٱللَّهَ يَـٰٓأُو۟لِى ٱلْأَلْبَـٰبِ لَعَلَّكُمْ تُفْلِحُونَ ﴿١٠٠﴾

Say, "The corrupt and the good are not equal, even though the abundance of (what is) corrupt may attract you. So, fear Allāh, O people of understanding, so that you may be successful." (Al-Mā'idah, 5:100)

The term *khabīth* applies to all forms of corrupt things, people, and ideas. When applied to things, the āyah means that a little wealth from ḥalāl sources is far better than a whole lot of it from ḥarām sources. Referring to this Sayyidnā Abū Hurayrah رضي الله عنه said, "One dirham from ḥalāl income that I give in charity is more beloved to me than a hundred thousand dirhams from ḥarām income." ʿUmar ibn ʿAbdul ʿAzīz invoked this āyah when government revenue was reduced considerably after his economic reforms that eliminated unjust taxes. Some functionaries were concerned about the running of the government. Not he. His response: Fill your rule with justice just as it was filled with injustice before, and Allāh will take care of us. Today we witness wholesale violation of this message in the running of everything from small organizations to big governments. We think that a hundred bucks are better than one, regardless of how they were earned.

The message is general and cautions us that in any situation we should not be swayed by numbers alone. This is the antidote to the tyranny of the majority and the claim to truth of the prevalent. We should never be the ones that go with the flow. We judge all things based on their own merit and not on their popularity or preponderance. Good is what Allāh declared to be good, no matter what the opinion polls say. Wrong is what He declared to be wrong, no matter how many pundits line up in its favor.

Self Reform

يَٰٓأَيُّهَا ٱلَّذِينَ ءَامَنُوا۟ عَلَيْكُمْ أَنفُسَكُمْ ۖ لَا يَضُرُّكُم مَّن ضَلَّ إِذَا ٱهْتَدَيْتُمْ ۚ
إِلَى ٱللَّهِ مَرْجِعُكُمْ جَمِيعًا فَيُنَبِّئُكُم بِمَا كُنتُمْ تَعْمَلُونَ ﴿١٠٥﴾

O you who believe, take care of your own selves. The one who has gone astray cannot harm you, if you are on the right path. To Allāh all of you have to return. Then He will tell you what you have been doing. (Al-Mā'idah, 5:105)

Our first responsibility is to reform ourselves for we will stand accountable to Allāh for our own actions and inactions, not of others.

Our normal conversations consist of criticizing others. This has a place in the proper scheme of things, when it is part of our conscious effort to promote good and prohibit evil and when it is guided by the Sharīʿah limits on such conversation. But when this becomes our sole occupation, to the exclusion of our self monitoring and accounting, there is a serious problem.

This is not a negation of our responsibility to enjoin good and forbid evil. Rather it assures us that when we have done our job in promoting good, yet people do not listen, then we will not be responsible for their actions. Saʿīd ibn al-Musayyab said: "When you have enjoined good and forbidden evil, and you are following the right path, then the going astray of a person despite your efforts will not harm you."

Denying Life after Death

وَقَالُوٓا۟ إِنْ هِىَ إِلَّا حَيَاتُنَا ٱلدُّنْيَا وَمَا نَحْنُ بِمَبْعُوثِينَ ﴿٢٩﴾ وَلَوْ تَرَىٰٓ إِذْ وُقِفُوا۟
عَلَىٰ رَبِّهِمْ ۚ قَالَ أَلَيْسَ هَـٰذَا بِٱلْحَقِّ ۚ قَالُوا۟ بَلَىٰ وَرَبِّنَا ۚ قَالَ فَذُوقُوا۟ ٱلْعَذَابَ بِمَا
كُنتُمْ تَكْفُرُونَ ﴿٣٠﴾

They say, "There is nothing but this worldly life of ours, and we are not going to be raised again." If only you could see when they will be made to stand before their Lord! He will say, "Is this not a reality?" They will say, "Of course, by our Lord, it is." He will say, "Then, taste the punishment, for you used to disbelieve." (Al-Anʿām 6:29-30)

This was revealed in Makkah and documents the belief of the pagans regarding the Afterlife.

The great intellectuals, scientists, professors, and authors of today who hold and promote this view are no better or different than the ignorant people of the pre-Islamic Jāhiliyyah society quoted here. All corruption arises from this basic premise that there is no life after this one. If this life is all there is to it, then might must be right because it works and moral principles are meaningless because they require you to give up immediate gratification and many a time go unrewarded in this world.

The second āyah tells us that visualizing the utter shock of those who subscribe to this view when they come face to face with reality after death is the best answer to their philosophies.

Limits on Interactions with the Non-Believers

وَإِذَا رَأَيْتَ ٱلَّذِينَ يَخُوضُونَ فِىٓ ءَايَٰتِنَا فَأَعْرِضْ عَنْهُمْ حَتَّىٰ يَخُوضُوا۟ فِى حَدِيثٍ غَيْرِهِۦ ۚ وَإِمَّا يُنسِيَنَّكَ ٱلشَّيْطَٰنُ فَلَا تَقْعُدْ بَعْدَ ٱلذِّكْرَىٰ مَعَ ٱلْقَوْمِ ٱلظَّٰلِمِينَ ﴿٦٨﴾

When you see men engaged in vain discourse about Our signs, turn away from them unless they turn to a different theme. If Satan ever makes you forget, then after recollection, sit not in the company of those who do wrong. (Al-Anʿām, 6:68)

This āyah sets the limits on interaction with the non-believers. If in any gathering, truth is ridiculed, blasphemy is perpetrated, or someone is making fun of Allāh and the Prophet, we must not sit in such company, watch or listen to such a program or participate in the chat. If we find ourselves in it, as soon as we realize it, we must show our disapproval by leaving. If this is isolationism then be it. We must isolate ourselves from evil environments for our own protection.

Juz Eight

Slick Talk

وَكَذَٰلِكَ جَعَلْنَا لِكُلِّ نَبِيٍّ عَدُوًّا شَيَٰطِينَ ٱلْإِنسِ وَٱلْجِنِّ يُوحِى
بَعْضُهُمْ إِلَىٰ بَعْضٍ زُخْرُفَ ٱلْقَوْلِ غُرُورًا ۚ وَلَوْ شَآءَ رَبُّكَ مَا فَعَلُوهُ ۖ فَذَرْهُمْ
وَمَا يَفْتَرُونَ ﴿١١٢﴾

So it is that, for every prophet, We have set up enemies—the devils of mankind and jinn—who whisper unto one another flowery discourses in order to deceive-Had Allāh willed, they would have not done it. So, leave them alone with what they forge. (Al-Anʿām, 6: 112)

The key phrase here is "*zukhraf al-qawl ghurūrā*" which can be translated as "embellished speech or varnished falsehood by way of deception." This is the slick talk that has been developed into perfection in the age of the media, sound bites, and spin doctors. These forces of deception will remain there; the task of the truth seeker is to be aware of their ways and not allow himself to be deceived by them.

The next āyah tells us that it is really those who do not believe in the Hereafter that will be persuaded by them. It says: "and (they seduce one another) in order that the hearts of those who do not believe in the Hereafter may incline to it."[1] A belief in the Hereafter that is alive and a concern for our accountability before the All-Knowing Allāh will protect us from their deceptions.

The Majority Says...

وَإِن تُطِعْ أَكْثَرَ مَن فِي ٱلْأَرْضِ يُضِلُّوكَ عَن سَبِيلِ ٱللَّهِ ۚ إِن يَتَّبِعُونَ
إِلَّا ٱلظَّنَّ وَإِنْ هُمْ إِلَّا يَخْرُصُونَ ﴿١١٦﴾

If you obey the majority of those on earth, they will make you lose the way of Allāh. They follow nothing but whims, and they do nothing but make conjectures. (Al-Anʿām 6:116)

This again emphasizes that matters of truth and falsehood cannot be decided through democracy or opinion polls. Further, the views of most people on fundamental questions of life are based on conjectures and speculation, not on certain knowledge, which can only come through revelation.

Inward and Outward Sins

وَذَرُوا۟ ظَٰهِرَ ٱلْإِثْمِ وَبَاطِنَهُۥٓ ۚ إِنَّ ٱلَّذِينَ يَكْسِبُونَ ٱلْإِثْمَ سَيُجْزَوْنَ
بِمَا كَانُوا۟ يَقْتَرِفُونَ ﴿١٢٠﴾

Forsake the outwardness of sin and the inwardness thereof. Lo! those who garner sin will be awarded that which they have earned. (Al-Anʿām 6:120)

---

1 *Al-Qur'ān*, al-Anʿām 6:113.

The outward sins are the content of our outward actions like telling lies, backbiting, failure to perform obligatory acts of worship, and failure to follow the commands of Allāh in all dealings and transactions. The inward sins are the thoughts, ideas and motives we hide in our heart like arrogance, malice, jealousy, and desire to show off.

The Islamic discipline of fiqh deals with the first; that of tasawwuf (although it is greatly misunderstood these days) deals with the second. The āyah makes it clear that both are important; reforming both our actions and our motives and thoughts are equal obligations.

Halal Slaughter

وَلَا تَأْكُلُوا۟ مِمَّا لَمْ يُذْكَرِ ٱسْمُ ٱللَّهِ عَلَيْهِ وَإِنَّهُۥ لَفِسْقٌ

Do not eat that (meat) over which the name of Allāh has not been pronounced. This is surely a sin. (Al-Anʿām 6:121)

Taking a life, even that of an animal that has been created to feed us, is something that we cannot do on our own authority. That is why it is of utmost importance that we slaughter that animal by pronouncing the name of Allāh and only in the way prescribed by Him. When the pronouncement is left out intentionally, or done by someone who does not believe in Allāh in the first place, then that meat is not permissible for consumption.

In this sūrah, which deals basically with the wrong beliefs of the mushrikeen of Makkah and is meant to explain and assert the truth of Islamic beliefs, it is interesting that the issue of ḥalāl and ḥarām meat has been discussed in no less than ten āyahs. This again makes it clear that this is not a secondary or peripheral issue.

Hearts, Open and Constricted

فَمَن يُرِدِ ٱللَّهُ أَن يَهْدِيَهُۥ يَشْرَحْ صَدْرَهُۥ لِلْإِسْلَـٰمِ ۖ وَمَن يُرِدْ أَن
يُضِلَّهُۥ يَجْعَلْ صَدْرَهُۥ ضَيِّقًا حَرَجًا كَأَنَّمَا يَصَّعَّدُ فِى ٱلسَّمَآءِ ۚ
كَذَٰلِكَ يَجْعَلُ ٱللَّهُ ٱلرِّجْسَ عَلَى ٱلَّذِينَ لَا يُؤْمِنُونَ ﴿١٢٥﴾

So, whomsoever Allāh wills to guide, He makes his heart wide open for Islam, and whomsoever He wills to let go astray, He makes his heart tight and constricted, (and he feels embracing Islam as difficult) as if he were climbing unto the skies. In this way, Allāh lays abomination on those who do not believe. (Al-Anʿām, 6:125)

A hadith explains the signs of this wide opening of the breast: "Turning to the eternal abode, turning away from the abode of deception (this world), and preparation for death before it comes."[2] Such a person would accept the commands of Allāh with an open heart.

There is much to ponder here for those Muslims who habitually show allergic reactions to different commands of the Sharīʿah. The roots of this behavior is the sickness of the heart mentioned here.

At higher elevations atmospheric pressure is low, making breathing difficult. (That is why airplane cabins are pressurized). What a fitting illustration of the constriction of the breast.

2 Abū Jaʿfar in *Muṣannaf ibn Abī Shaybah*, كتاب الزهد [Book: Zuhd], no. 34314.

A Muslim's Pledge

قُلْ إِنَّ صَلَاتِي وَنُسُكِي وَمَحْيَايَ وَمَمَاتِي لِلَّهِ رَبِّ الْعَالَمِينَ ﴿١٦٢﴾ لَا
شَرِيكَ لَهُ ۖ وَبِذَٰلِكَ أُمِرْتُ وَأَنَا أَوَّلُ الْمُسْلِمِينَ ﴿١٦٣﴾

Say, my worship and my sacrifice and my living and my dying are for Allāh, Lord of the Worlds. For Him there is no partner. And thus I have been commanded, and I am the first one to submit." (Al-Anʿām 6:162-163)

This is the definition of the Muslim—one who surrenders completely and as a result loves and hates; and lives and dies for the sake of Allāh. As the Qur'ān explains in several places, this was the call of all the previous prophets as well.[3]

Dress Code

يَا بَنِي آدَمَ قَدْ أَنزَلْنَا عَلَيْكُمْ لِبَاسًا يُوَارِي سَوْآتِكُمْ وَرِيشًا ۖ وَلِبَاسُ التَّقْوَىٰ
ذَٰلِكَ خَيْرٌ ۚ ذَٰلِكَ مِنْ آيَاتِ اللَّهِ لَعَلَّهُمْ يَذَّكَّرُونَ ﴿٢٦﴾

O Children of Adam! We have bestowed raiment upon you to cover your shame, as well as to be an adornment to you. But the raiment of righteousness,- that is the best. Such are among the Signs of Allāh, that they may receive admonition! (Al-Aʿrāf, 7:26)

While all other animals have a skin that provides them protection against the elements, human beings don't. Monkeys can live without clothing; human beings cannot. Why? It is not that our bodies did not develop our skin—so thin and fur free that it requires external covering for protection—because of some unexplained evolutionary accident. Rather, our

3 See for example, Al-Baqarah 2:131-132, al-Mā'idah 5:111, Yūnus 10:72, Yūnus 10:84, Yūsuf 12:101, al-Ambiyā' 21:25.

Creator designed it this way so we will always need clothing. He also put in us the sense of shame that forces us to cover ourselves. At the same time, He provided us with the means and abilities for producing nice clothes. On the other hand, the first act of Satan was to cause Adam and Eve to expose themselves as explained in the āyahs preceding this one.

The address here is to all humanity, emphasizing thereby the universal human need to cover ourselves properly. The Qur'ān then warns that Satan was not finished after his first attempt for the next āyah says: "Oh Children of Adam! Let not Satan seduce you in the same manner as he got your parents out of the Garden, stripping them of their raiment, to expose their shame."[4]

Those who design, promote, and use the fashions—especially women's fashions—that develop new ways of *not* covering the body are thus obedient servants of Satan, whether they realize it or not.

Homosexuality

وَلُوطًا إِذْ قَالَ لِقَوْمِهِۦٓ أَتَأْتُونَ ٱلْفَـٰحِشَةَ مَا سَبَقَكُم بِهَا مِنْ أَحَدٍ مِّنَ ٱلْعَـٰلَمِينَ ﴿٨٠﴾ إِنَّكُمْ لَتَأْتُونَ ٱلرِّجَالَ شَهْوَةً مِّن دُونِ ٱلنِّسَآءِ ۚ بَلْ أَنتُمْ قَوْمٌ مُّسْرِفُونَ ﴿٨١﴾

And (remember) Lūṭ, when he said unto his people: "Do you commit abominations such as none in all the world has ever done before you? Verily, with lust you approach men instead of women. You are indeed a people transgressing beyond bounds." (Al-A'rāf, 7:80-81)

The story of the people of Prophet Lūṭ (Lot) عليه السلام is mentioned in more than ten sūrahs in the Qur'ān. This is a story of crime, defiance, and punishment. Unprecedented crime, extremism

4 *Al-Qur'ān*, al-A'rāf 7:27.

in insisting on that crime, and exemplary punishment. Anyone who reads this narrative with an open mind can have not the slightest confusion about Islam's attitude about homosexuality.

The first thing the Qur'ān mentions is that homosexual practice was invented by the people to whom Prophet Lūṭ عليه السلام was sent as a messenger. The Qur'ānic word is *al-fāḥishah*, which means lewdness, shameful act, indecency. Fornication and adultery (*zinā*) are also mentioned as examples of *fāḥishah* in the Qur'ān.[5] But here the definite article *al* is added to show the even more serious nature of this act. Homosexual act is not *fāḥishah* but *al-fāḥishah*. It is not just a shameful act but the shameful act, the lewdness, the abomination.

Secondly in telling that no one before them committed this act, the Qur'ān uses the word *min* in addition to *aḥadin*. Without this, it would still mean that no one did it before you. But with *min* emphasis is added. In other words, no one whosoever ever did this act among all the creatures. This is an outright rejection of the claim that this tendency is an inborn and ingrained part of nature for which no person should be held accountable. Prophet Lūṭ عليه السلام accuses them of having invented this shameful act. And the Sodomites do not say that they are helpless because it is a call of nature. Rather they say, "You know very well what we *want*."[6] And that the Prophet عليه السلام would be added to the list of people who have been expelled from their city for objecting to their practices if he does not cease and desist from criticizing their way of life.[7] They are the inventors of this perversion and fully committed to use of violence to defend it.

This Qur'ānic account regarding the genesis of this perversion is attested to not only by the Bible and the Talmud

---

5 *Al-Qur'ān*, al-Isrā' 17:32.

6 *Al-Qur'ān*, Hūd 11:79.

7 *Al-Qur'ān*, al-Shuʿarā' 26:167.

but also by the terms used to describe this act in languages around the world. It is sodomy in English, sodomie and sodomiser (the doer) in French, sodomia and sodomizar in Spanish and sodomi in Norwegian. Sodomie in German and sodomia in Polish also refer to variant forms of sexual perversion. All point to the fact that it was invented in Sodom, which was the principle city of these people. In Arabic and languages influenced by it like Urdu the term used is liwatat or aml qaum lut, referring to the practice of the people of Prophet Lūṭ عليه السلام. Again it is pointing to the same date and place of invention.

The date is about four thousand years ago. For thousands of years before that no one ever felt the urge for this perversion. Obviously if it was in human nature then some people in earlier times should also have expressed this inclination. The place is the area now submerged under the Dead Sea. This was a very prosperous and rich fertile land. Then the punishment came in the form of a huge earthquake and rain of brimstones and fires that turned their world upside down. The area then became the lowest point on the face of the earth, being about 1300 feet below sea level. It was submerged under the ocean and turned into a desolate place where little life exists. Its harsh environment permits neither fish or other sea animals nor aquatic plants. It was as the Qur'ān said: "And verily of that We have left a clear sign for people who have sense." [8]

Sodomites committed other crimes as well like highway robbery and performing shameful acts in public as mentioned in one place in the Qur'ān[9] But their biggest crime was homosexuality, which is mentioned repeatedly. And then there was defiance. When Prophet Lūṭ عليه السلام warned them about divine retribution, they challenged him to bring it

8 *Al-Qur'ān*, al-ʿAnkabūt 29:35.

9 *Al-Qur'ān*, al-ʿAnkabūt 29:29.

on. [10] Their fate was thus sealed by their own demand. That was before the angels arrived at the scene. Their invasion of the house of Prophet Lūṭ ﷺ for the explicit purpose of molesting the angels who appeared in the guise of beautiful young men was thus just the last nail in their coffin. It was not the primary reason for their punishment.

Some people have tried to distort the Qur'ānic account by claiming that their crime was rape not homosexuality. Others have surmised that the problem was that they were targeting young children, otherwise it would be fine. The Qur'ān does not leave the slightest possibility of such interpretation. In the āyah quoted above it says: "Verily, with lust you approach men instead of women." It is *rijāl* (men) not *aṭfāl* (children). It is for the act itself, without any mention of compulsion, that they are called as *musrifūn* (going beyond limits).

Also significant is the role of Prophet Lūṭ's ﷺ wife. While in the entire town only one house was saved, that of Prophet Lūṭ ﷺ, even in that house there was an exception. It was the wife of the Prophet, who was killed with the rest of the people. Her fate is mentioned repeatedly so it does not remain just a footnote to the story. Why was she punished? Not for committing homosexual acts but for betraying her husband.[11] She betrayed the cause of her husband by being an active sympathizer with the people and therefore shared their fate.

When the people invaded the house of Prophet Lūṭ ﷺ, and he was at the point of despair, the people were blinded by the angels.[12] We can see a figurative blindness in the people who try to make a case for approval of homosexuality in Islam. A most bizarre argument that has been forwarded by some of them is that the Qur'ān mentions the presence

10 *Al-Qur'ān*, al-ʿAnkabūt 29:29.
11 *Al-Qur'ān*, al-Taḥrīm 66:10.
12 *Al-Qur'ān*, al-Qamar 54:35.

of young boys as servants in Paradise. Interestingly it is the same people who argue that the modern homosexual affair is between consenting adults and that they also agree that sex with young boys is wrong. Yet that is what comes to their lustful minds when they read the accounts of the servants in the Qur'ān.

If they had maintained their sensibilities, they would have realized that this Qur'ānic account actually gives exactly the opposite message. In Paradise women will not be in the public places. They will be in the private space, where they will not face the attention of anyone except their husbands ("houris, cloistered in cool pavilions"[13]). Young boys will be in all the public places, because those who enter Paradise will not look at them with any sexual desires. They will have nothing to worry as those who could look at them with desire will not be in Paradise at all. They will be in the exact opposite of Paradise, a small manifestation of which was given to the people of Prophet Lūṭ عليه السلام.

Self-Righteousness

وَمَا كَانَ جَوَابَ قَوْمِهِۦٓ إِلَّآ أَن قَالُوٓاْ أَخْرِجُوهُم مِّن قَرْيَتِكُمْ ۖ إِنَّهُمْ أُنَاسٌ يَتَطَهَّرُونَ ﴿٨٢﴾

But his people's only answer was this: "Expel them (Lūṭ and his followers) from your township! Verily, they are folk who make themselves out to be pure!" (Al-Aʿrāf, 7:82)

The people of Prophet Lūṭ عليه السلام not only invented the heinous practice of homosexuality, they also fashioned a propaganda weapon for fighting those who would try to stop them. As

13 *Al-Qur'ān*, al-Raḥmān 55:72.

quoted above they blamed Prophet Lūṭ ﷺ and his associates of being self-righteous.

We can hear the echoes of this blame even today. If someone dares to say that what someone else is saying or doing is wrong or un-Islamic, he will be immediately convicted of being self-righteous. And there is no sin greater than that. With this one word anyone can be stopped from pointing out any wrongs.

Needless to say the term does not belong in the Islamic discourse. Muslims have had lots of debates in their history on the actions and words of each other. But you do not find the use of this word in these debates. The proper response to an accusation of wrongdoing is to show that the act in question is not wrong. But those using a counter accusation of self-righteousness are in effect saying: "How dare you accuse us of doing anything wrong." Instead of answering the accusation, they aim at silencing it. So we should make it clear that the term is not acceptable in the Islamic discourse. In fact the entire institution of *amr bil maʿrūf wa nahi ʿanil munkar*, so central to Islam, can be disbanded if we continue to allow the use of this term.

Juz Nine

Hardships and Ease

وَمَآ أَرۡسَلۡنَا فِي قَرۡيَةٖ مِّن نَّبِيٍّ إِلَّآ أَخَذۡنَآ أَهۡلَهَا بِٱلۡبَأۡسَآءِ وَٱلضَّرَّآءِ
لَعَلَّهُمۡ يَضَّرَّعُونَ ﴿٩٤﴾ ثُمَّ بَدَّلۡنَا مَكَانَ ٱلسَّيِّئَةِ ٱلۡحَسَنَةَ حَتَّىٰ عَفَواْ
وَّقَالُواْ قَدۡ مَسَّ ءَابَآءَنَا ٱلضَّرَّآءُ وَٱلسَّرَّآءُ فَأَخَذۡنَٰهُم بَغۡتَةٗ وَهُمۡ لَا
يَشۡعُرُونَ ﴿٩٥﴾

We did not send any prophet to a town, but We seized its people with hardship and suffering, so that they might humble themselves; then We transformed the affliction into ease of life, so that they thrived and said (to themselves), "Misfortune and hardship befell our forefathers as well"—whereupon We took them to task, all of a sudden, without their being aware (of what was coming). (Al-Aʿrāf, 7:94-95)

This sūrah narrated stories of many Messengers whose nations refused to listen to them and were ultimately destroyed. Here is then a general statement about their behavior. The hardships and ease of life were created by Allāh as a way of shaking them out of their complacency with their ignorant ways. They are not accidents that just happen randomly, nor are they ultimately the result of just the local and apparent causes. There is a Divine plan behind everything that is happening in the world. People of wisdom can see the Hand of Allāh in their afflictions as well as their prosperity and use both to come closer to Him and to submit to Him. Others fail—even refuse—to see it that way and are destroyed. This is a very important reminder for developing the right outlook about the news of the day.

Blind Imitation

وَجَٰوَزۡنَا بِبَنِيٓ إِسۡرَٰٓءِيلَ ٱلۡبَحۡرَ فَأَتَوۡاْ عَلَىٰ قَوۡمٖ يَعۡكُفُونَ عَلَىٰٓ أَصۡنَامٖ لَّهُمۡۚ
قَالُواْ يَٰمُوسَى ٱجۡعَل لَّنَآ إِلَٰهٗا كَمَا لَهُمۡ ءَالِهَةٞۚ قَالَ إِنَّكُمۡ قَوۡمٞ تَجۡهَلُونَ
١٣٨ إِنَّ هَٰٓؤُلَآءِ مُتَبَّرٞ مَّا هُمۡ فِيهِ وَبَٰطِلٞ مَّا كَانُواْ يَعۡمَلُونَ ١٣٩

We made the children of Isrā'īl cross the sea, then they came across a people sitting in devotion before their idols. They (the Israelites) said, "O Mūsā, make a god for us like they have gods." He said, "You are really an ignorant people. What these people are engaged in is sure to be destroyed; and false is what they are doing." (Al-Aʿrāf, 7:138-139)

This is after the Israelites had been rescued from the Pharaoh's oppression. Long years of slavery had taken their toll on their ways of thinking and this can be seen in the slavish mentality showcased here. Blind imitation of the other (as can be seen in the vast areas of the Muslim world today regarding the West) is a serious disease. We want the same objects of devotion, days of celebration, and pursuits and patterns of life as those who we think to be successful.

Ibn ʿAṭiyyah says, the children of Israel perhaps were not proposing idol worship per se; they might have been rationalizing that the statue would help them visualize and thereby do their worship of God with more concentration. If true, it only shows that such rationalizations camouflaging a slavish mentality—so common today as a result of colonial experience—have a long history. Let us not forget that the children of Israel did end up doing calf worship after all.

In any case the reply of Prophet Mūsā ﵇ is so fitting and it can help rid us of this debilitating sickness.

The Prophet and His True Followers

ٱلَّذِينَ يَتَّبِعُونَ ٱلرَّسُولَ ٱلنَّبِيَّ ٱلْأُمِّيَّ ٱلَّذِى يَجِدُونَهُۥ مَكْتُوبًا
عِندَهُمْ فِى ٱلتَّوْرَىٰةِ وَٱلْإِنجِيلِ يَأْمُرُهُم بِٱلْمَعْرُوفِ وَيَنْهَىٰهُمْ
عَنِ ٱلْمُنكَرِ وَيُحِلُّ لَهُمُ ٱلطَّيِّبَٰتِ وَيُحَرِّمُ عَلَيْهِمُ ٱلْخَبَٰٓئِثَ
وَيَضَعُ عَنْهُمْ إِصْرَهُمْ وَٱلْأَغْلَٰلَ ٱلَّتِى كَانَتْ عَلَيْهِمْ ۚ فَٱلَّذِينَ
ءَامَنُوا۟ بِهِۦ وَعَزَّرُوهُ وَنَصَرُوهُ وَٱتَّبَعُوا۟ ٱلنُّورَ ٱلَّذِىٓ أُنزِلَ مَعَهُۥٓ ۙ أُو۟لَٰٓئِكَ
هُمُ ٱلْمُفْلِحُونَ ﴿١٥٧﴾

Those who follow the Messenger, the Ummī (unlettered) prophet whom they find mentioned in their own (scriptures), in the Torah (law) and the Injīl (Gospel), and who bids them what is fair and forbids what is unfair, and makes lawful for them good things, and makes unlawful for them impure things, and relieves them of their burden, and of the shackles that were upon them. So, those who believe in him and support him, and help him and follow the light sent down with him, those are the ones who are successful. (Al-Aʿrāf, 7:157)

This is a concise introduction to Prophet Muḥammad ﷺ and his message. He commands what is fair, just, and good. He forbids what is unfair, unjust, and evil. He declares permissible what is clean and pure. He declares impermissible what is unclean and unhealthy. He liberates humanity from the shackles that it had put upon itself—those of customs, traditions, superstitions and man-made laws. His is the most empowering and liberating message that leads to eternal success. This success is only for those who reject all the competing heroes and exemplars for the light of guidance brought by him.

The Sabbath-Breakers

وَسْـَٔلْهُمْ عَنِ ٱلْقَرْيَةِ ٱلَّتِى كَانَتْ حَاضِرَةَ ٱلْبَحْرِ إِذْ
يَعْدُونَ فِى ٱلسَّبْتِ إِذْ تَأْتِيهِمْ حِيتَانُهُمْ يَوْمَ سَبْتِهِمْ
شُرَّعًا وَيَوْمَ لَا يَسْبِتُونَ لَا تَأْتِيهِمْ كَذَٰلِكَ نَبْلُوهُم بِمَا
كَانُوا۟ يَفْسُقُونَ ﴿١٦٣﴾

Ask them about the town which stood by the sea, when they used to transgress in the matter of Sabbath, when their fish came to them openly on the Sabbath, and did not come when they did not have Sabbath. In this way, We put them to a test, because they used to act sinfully. (Al-Aʿrāf, 7:163)

Muhammad Asad writes: "The story of the Sabbath-breakers (alluded to in several places in the Qur'ān) is a general illustration of the tendency, so often manifested by the children of Israel, to offend against their religious laws in pursuit of their passions or for the sake of worldly gain."[1]

1 This is not to say that the specific incidents mentioned in tafsīrs are not true. But the point is that it was their general attitude.

Unfortunately the description of the past of the children of Israel fits the present of much of the Muslim world with all sorts of economic justifications being offered for putting Allāh's commands on the side. Those who put forward or accept such fancy justifications, sometimes in highly academic language, should realize that when economic gains result from breaking Allāh's commands, then the situation is itself a punishment for our transgressions. And the proper thing to do is to throw away the balance sheets and turn to Allāh in repentance.

Innate Sense of the Creator

وَإِذْ أَخَذَ رَبُّكَ مِنۢ بَنِىٓ ءَادَمَ مِن ظُهُورِهِمْ ذُرِّيَّتَهُمْ وَأَشْهَدَهُمْ عَلَىٰٓ أَنفُسِهِمْ أَلَسْتُ بِرَبِّكُمْ ۖ قَالُوا۟ بَلَىٰ ۛ شَهِدْنَآ ۛ أَن تَقُولُوا۟ يَوْمَ ٱلْقِيَـٰمَةِ إِنَّا كُنَّا عَنْ هَـٰذَا غَـٰفِلِينَ ﴿١٧٢﴾

(Recall) when your Lord brought forth their progeny from the loins of the children of Ādam, and made them testify about themselves (by asking them,) "Am I not your Lord?" They said, "Of course, You are. We testify." (We did so) lest you should say on the Day of Judgment, "We were unaware of this." (Al-Aʿrāf, 7:163)

According to the Qur'ān, as explained further by several ahadith, all human beings who will be born until the Last Day had a prior existence when the witnessing referred to above took place. Our innate sense of our Creator and our obligation to worship and obey Him is a result of that event. That is why belief in a deity and acts of worship have been a common phenomenon in all human societies. Another hadith informs us that all human beings are born in the state of *fiṭrah*, which is in perfect harmony with Islam, and only later parents and environmental influences make them deviate from that path.

The awareness may be obscured from our conscience and buried deeply under false ideas but it comes to the surface at extraordinary times. Thus at times of great calamities people of all persuasions suddenly remember God.

The Prophet and the Knowledge of the Unseen

قُل لَّآ أَمۡلِكُ لِنَفۡسِي نَفۡعٗا وَلَا ضَرًّا إِلَّا مَا شَآءَ ٱللَّهُۚ وَلَوۡ كُنتُ أَعۡلَمُ
ٱلۡغَيۡبَ لَٱسۡتَكۡثَرۡتُ مِنَ ٱلۡخَيۡرِ وَمَا مَسَّنِيَ ٱلسُّوٓءُۚ إِنۡ أَنَا۠ إِلَّا نَذِيرٞ
وَبَشِيرٞ لِّقَوۡمٖ يُؤۡمِنُونَ ١٨٨

Say, "I have no power to bring a benefit or a harm to myself, except that which Allāh wills. If I had the knowledge of the Unseen, I would have accumulated a lot of good things, and no evil would have ever touched me. I am but a warner, and a herald of good news for a people who believe." (Al-Aʿrāf, 7:188)

Prophets receive communications from God and speak to the people for Him, but they are not God. Many people have difficulty in comprehending this distinction. Non-believers, including the mushrikeen of the pre-Islamic Jāhiliyyah said that if the Prophet did not have divine powers then he could not be the Prophet. Ignorant followers later claimed that he indeed had full knowledge of the unseen. This āyah sets the record straight. The Prophet is a human being, but he is appointed by Allāh to speak for Him to humanity. His knowledge of the unseen world exceeds that of other human beings, because it has been given to him by Allāh. But this is not the all encompassing knowledge of the unseen, which is held by no one except Allāh.

Listening to the Qur'ān

وَإِذَا قُرِئَ ٱلْقُرْءَانُ فَٱسْتَمِعُوا۟ لَهُۥ وَأَنصِتُوا۟ لَعَلَّكُمْ تُرْحَمُونَ ﴿٢٠٤﴾

When the Qur'ān is recited, hearken unto it, and listen in silence, so that you may be blessed. (Al-Aʿrāf 7:204)

This is the proper etiquette regarding Qur'ānic recitation. The Qur'ān should command our attention and devotion unlike any other word, as this is the Word of Allāh. Disrespect here will deprive us of the mercy contained in it. Consequently a person should not recite it audibly at a place where people are busy in other activities and will not be able to listen to it attentively. Unfortunately in the media age this situation has become more common. Electronic devices make recitation easy but many a time the required attention is lacking. We should remember that the Qur'ānic recitation should never form the background sound for our activities. We should either listen to it with full attention or turn it off. For the same reason using it as a ring toner in mobile phones is an act of disrespect.

When the Qur'ān is recited in tarāwīh, the spirit of this āyah requires that we listen to it and not leave in the middle without a good reason. Even worse would be to engage in socializing and ignore the recitation of the Qur'ān. Unfortunately these are becoming a common trend in our communities, and especially amongst the youth in the West.

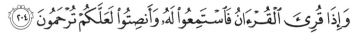

Juz Ten

Nurturing Īmān Before Issuing Commands

This juz begins with the following āyah:

وَٱعْلَمُوٓاْ أَنَّمَا غَنِمْتُم مِّن شَىْءٍ فَأَنَّ لِلَّهِ خُمُسَهُۥ وَلِلرَّسُولِ وَلِذِى ٱلْقُرْبَىٰ وَٱلْيَتَـٰمَىٰ وَٱلْمَسَـٰكِينِ وَٱبْنِ ٱلسَّبِيلِ إِن كُنتُمْ ءَامَنتُم بِٱللَّهِ وَمَآ أَنزَلْنَا عَلَىٰ عَبْدِنَا يَوْمَ ٱلْفُرْقَانِ يَوْمَ ٱلْتَقَى ٱلْجَمْعَانِ وَٱللَّهُ عَلَىٰ كُلِّ شَىْءٍ قَدِيرٌ ﴿٤١﴾

And know that whatever spoils you receive, their one fifth is for Allāh and for His Messenger, and for kinsmen and orphans and the needy and the wayfarer, if you do believe in Allāh and in what We sent down upon Our Servant on the Decisive Day, the day when the two forces encountered each other. And Allāh is powerful over everything. (Al-Anfāl, 8:41)

This is an answer to the question which was mentioned right in the beginning of sūrah al-Anfāl itself, forty āyahs ago. That āyah said:

"They ask you about the spoils. Say, "The spoils are for Allāh and the Messenger." So, fear Allāh, and set your relations right, and obey Allāh and His Messenger, if you are believers."[1]

The question was about the distribution of the spoils of war. In the tribal society the soldier who laid his hand on the spoil kept it. The rules were to be changed now. But it is extremely significant that after mentioning the question, the answer was delayed while mention was made of the special favors of Allāh that led to the decisive victory in the highly unequal battle of Badr for which Muslims were not even prepared. Mention was also made of the qualities of the true believers, whose hearts tremble upon the mention of the name of Allāh, whose īmān increases upon listening to the Words of Allāh, and who put their trust in Him.

The ruling regarding distribution was given after the minds had been prepared to accept it. Today a mention of rulings—in all areas of life—elicits arguments instead of compliance because of the lack of this preparation. Unless Islamic education carefully nurtures īmān and creates strong conviction about Islamic beliefs and teachings, simply imparting knowledge of commandments will not change the behavior. Today the sources of this nurture are neither in the formal education nor in the environment created by the media. Parents and educators can continue to ignore this point only with disastrous results.

---

1 *Al-Qur'ān*, al-Anfāl 8:1.

The Wealth of the Hypocrites

فَلَا تُعْجِبْكَ أَمْوَٰلُهُمْ وَلَآ أَوْلَـٰدُهُمْ ۚ إِنَّمَا يُرِيدُ ٱللَّهُ لِيُعَذِّبَهُم بِهَا فِى
ٱلْحَيَوٰةِ ٱلدُّنْيَا وَتَزْهَقَ أَنفُسُهُمْ وَهُمْ كَـٰفِرُونَ ٥٥

Let not, then, their wealth and their children excite your admiration. In fact, Allāh intends to punish them with these in this lowly life and that their souls should depart while they are disbelievers. (At-Tawbah, 9:55, 85)

Sūrah Tawbah contains much commentary about the hypocrites. This āyah is also about them. The hypocrites were men of wealth and position. In fact their possessions, and their undue love for them, were the main cause of their hypocrisy. This āyah reminds us that the wealth of a hypocrite or non-believer should never engender envy in the believer. We must not be dazzled by the lifestyles of the rich and famous. Net worth estimates should not excite us. Accounts of the richest men should not attract us. If we realize the troubles in the Hereafter caused by disbelief, we'll feel pity rather than envy.

Hypocrites versus Believers

ٱلْمُنَـٰفِقُونَ وَٱلْمُنَـٰفِقَـٰتُ بَعْضُهُم مِّنۢ بَعْضٍ ۚ يَأْمُرُونَ
بِٱلْمُنكَرِ وَيَنْهَوْنَ عَنِ ٱلْمَعْرُوفِ وَيَقْبِضُونَ أَيْدِيَهُمْ ۚ نَسُوا۟
ٱللَّهَ فَنَسِيَهُمْ ۗ إِنَّ ٱلْمُنَـٰفِقِينَ هُمُ ٱلْفَـٰسِقُونَ ٦٧

The hypocrites, males and females, are all alike. They enjoin vice and forbid virtue and withhold their hands (from doing good). They are oblivious of Allāh, and so He is oblivious of them. Surely, the hypocrites are the sinners. (At-Tawbah, 9: 67)

وَٱلْمُؤْمِنُونَ وَٱلْمُؤْمِنَٰتُ بَعْضُهُمْ أَوْلِيَآءُ بَعْضٍ ۚ يَأْمُرُونَ بِٱلْمَعْرُوفِ
وَيَنْهَوْنَ عَنِ ٱلْمُنكَرِ وَيُقِيمُونَ ٱلصَّلَوٰةَ وَيُؤْتُونَ ٱلزَّكَوٰةَ
وَيُطِيعُونَ ٱللَّهَ وَرَسُولَهُۥٓ ۚ أُو۟لَٰٓئِكَ سَيَرْحَمُهُمُ ٱللَّهُ ۗ إِنَّ ٱللَّهَ عَزِيزٌ
حَكِيمٌ ﴿٧١﴾

The believers, male and female, are protectors one of another: they enjoin virtue and forbid vice and establish Ṣalāh and pay Zakāh and obey Allāh and His Messenger. On them will Allāh pour His mercy. Surely, Allāh is Powerful, Wise. (At-Tawbah, 9: 71)

These two verses compare and contrast believers and hypocrites and invite deep reflection.

More often than we realize we are engaged in persuading others or are being persuaded by them about big and small things in life. It is a very powerful force. That is why marketers yearn for word of mouth publicity and powerful media machines long for becoming the talk of the town.

Concerned with good as it is, Islam gives this tremendous social force a purpose. It must be used for promoting good, truth and justice and checking evil and injustice. That is the essence of *amr bil maʿrūf wa nahi ʿanil munkar*. And the Qur'ān declares it as the defining mission for this Ummah.

A believer may commit sins, but he cannot be on the side of promoting them. In the Islamic society sin is a private weakness, not a public cause.

Today we seem to be doing exactly the opposite. There are Muslim women who have been pressured out of observing hijab by friends and relatives. Men and women are enticed into riba transactions by family and friends. All innovations (bidʿah) and false social practices continue under social pressures. Bribery, backbiting, corruption, indecency, and dishonesty flourish under social approval. It is frightening to see how our real life matches the description given for the hypocrites. For we are warned that if we persuade others to commit a wrong we'll add to our burden of sins by the same amount. It is one thing to commit a wrong out of weakness. It is totally different to advocate the wrong and willingly multiply our burden of sins.

Juz Eleven

Sin, Repentance, and Forgiveness

وَءَاخَرُونَ ٱعْتَرَفُوا۟ بِذُنُوبِهِمْ خَلَطُوا۟ عَمَلًا صَٰلِحًا وَءَاخَرَ سَيِّئًا عَسَى ٱللَّهُ أَن
يَتُوبَ عَلَيْهِمْ ۚ إِنَّ ٱللَّهَ غَفُورٌ رَّحِيمٌ ﴿١٠٢﴾

And there are others who admitted their sins while they had mixed a good deed with an evil one. It is likely that Allāh will relent towards them. Surely, Allāh is Most-Forgiving, Very-Merciful. (At-Tawbah 9:102)

This is part of the commentary of the Qur'ān on the Tabūk expedition. It was an extraordinary time. The Islamic state faced a grave threat from the Roman army, which represented a superpower of the time. A call for universal mobilization was thus given. The hypocrites failed to respond. But some true Muslims also failed to show up. What separated these ten people from the rest was their later behavior. The hypocrites fabricated excuses for their failure. The true believers admitted their mistake without hesitation. Out of these, seven Companions tied themselves to the pillars in the Masjid Nabawi as an act of self punishment. These are mentioned here and forgiveness for them is announced. Three others did not submit themselves to this self-punishment but acknowledged their error when the Prophet ﷺ returned. They were subjected to a severe social boycott for fifty days before they were forgiven.

The hypocrites did not get any punishment. But their eternal punishment in the Hereafter was announced here.

We all make mistakes. What distinguishes a true believer from a hypocrite is not the absence of sin, even major sin, but the moral courage to admit it and sincere desire to reform. A true believer would never try to rationalize or justify his sins, leave alone insist on them.

Boundaries Set by Allāh

ٱلتَّٰٓئِبُونَ ٱلْعَٰبِدُونَ ٱلْحَٰمِدُونَ ٱلسَّٰٓئِحُونَ
ٱلرَّٰكِعُونَ ٱلسَّٰجِدُونَ ٱلْـَٔامِرُونَ بِٱلْمَعْرُوفِ
وَٱلنَّاهُونَ عَنِ ٱلْمُنكَرِ وَٱلْحَٰفِظُونَ لِحُدُودِ ٱللَّهِ ۗ وَبَشِّرِ
ٱلْمُؤْمِنِينَ ١١٢

(Triumphant) are those who turn repentant (to Allāh), those who serve (Him), those who praise (Him), those who fast, those who bow down, those who fall prostrate (in worship), those who enjoin the right and who forbid the wrong and those who keep (within) the boundaries (set by) Allāh—And give glad tidings to believers! (At-Tawbah 9:112)

These are the qualities of the true believers who were being contrasted with the hypocrites in this sūrah. Each of these qualities demands serious introspection so we can see where we stand.

"Keeping within the boundaries" requires a word of explanation. Our life is a complex web of relations and interactions involving ourselves, the world around us, and our Creator. We are subject to conflicting demands and emotions regarding all of them. To achieve a perfect balance in this complex situation is a lifelong struggle. The key to success in this struggle is being fully cognizant of the boundaries set by Allāh. For example, our spouses have rights on us, as do our parents. They may sometimes also come into conflict. Earning a ḥalāl living is a sacred duty. It can at times also interfere with our other obligations. Serving humanity is a noble act. What if it causes one to neglect his duties toward Allāh? In all these cases the fair resolution of the conflict requires that we not exceed the limits set by Allāh in each relationship. Learning the limits, and learning to stick by them in real life, is itself a lifelong effort. We should know where the lines are drawn in each situation and make our best effort not to cross them. But only those can have some hope of succeeding in this effort who are aware of the task itself.

Education

وَمَا كَانَ ٱلْمُؤْمِنُونَ لِيَنفِرُوا۟ كَآفَّةً ۚ فَلَوْلَا نَفَرَ مِن كُلِّ فِرْقَةٍ مِّنْهُمْ
طَآئِفَةٌ لِّيَتَفَقَّهُوا۟ فِى ٱلدِّينِ وَلِيُنذِرُوا۟ قَوْمَهُمْ إِذَا رَجَعُوٓا۟ إِلَيْهِمْ
لَعَلَّهُمْ يَحْذَرُونَ ١٢٢

Nor should the Believers all go forth together (in time of war): if a contingent from every expedition remained behind, they could devote themselves to studies in religion, and admonish the people when they return to them—that thus they (may learn) to guard themselves (against evil). (At-Tawbah 9:122)

The Tabūk expedition required a general mobilization where everyone was required to go with the army. Here it is made clear that this was the exception and not the rule. Even during war, there is another very important task that the community collectively has to be aware of. This is the task of Islamic education.

The purpose of Islamic education, as laid out here, is to provide that knowledge, guidance, and inspiration that is needed by the community of believers to guard itself from all harmful and un-Islamic practices and continue its journey of life on the Straight Path.

This āyah is the foundation stone upon which the entire structure of Islamic education is to be built. All talk of education in the Muslim world that is not informed by this āyah is misguided and a waste—as is happening today.

Calls to Revise the Qur'ān

وَإِذَا تُتْلَىٰ عَلَيْهِمْ ءَايَاتُنَا بَيِّنَٰتٍ ۙ قَالَ ٱلَّذِينَ لَا يَرْجُونَ لِقَآءَنَا
ٱئْتِ بِقُرْءَانٍ غَيْرِ هَٰذَآ أَوْ بَدِّلْهُ ۚ قُلْ مَا يَكُونُ لِىٓ أَنْ أُبَدِّلَهُۥ مِن
تِلْقَآئِ نَفْسِىٓ ۖ إِنْ أَتَّبِعُ إِلَّا مَا يُوحَىٰٓ إِلَىَّ ۖ إِنِّىٓ أَخَافُ إِنْ عَصَيْتُ
رَبِّى عَذَابَ يَوْمٍ عَظِيمٍ ﴿١٥﴾

And when Our clear āyahs are recited unto them they who look not for the meeting with Us say: Bring a Qur'ān other than this, or change it. Say (O Muḥammad): It is not for me to change it of my own accord. I only follow that which is revealed to me. Lo! If I disobey my Lord I fear the retribution of an awful Day. (Yūnus 10:15)

The calls to "reform" or revise the Qur'ān keep coming to this day. Sometimes they use the euphemism of reinterpretation for revision. There is nothing modern or novel about them. Their motive is the same, and our answer is the same as given here.

The Reality of This Life

إِنَّمَا مَثَلُ ٱلْحَيَوٰةِ ٱلدُّنْيَا كَمَآءٍ أَنزَلْنَٰهُ مِنَ ٱلسَّمَآءِ فَٱخْتَلَطَ بِهِۦ نَبَاتُ
ٱلْأَرْضِ مِمَّا يَأْكُلُ ٱلنَّاسُ وَٱلْأَنْعَٰمُ حَتَّىٰٓ إِذَآ أَخَذَتِ ٱلْأَرْضُ زُخْرُفَهَا
وَٱزَّيَّنَتْ وَظَنَّ أَهْلُهَآ أَنَّهُمْ قَٰدِرُونَ عَلَيْهَآ أَتَىٰهَآ أَمْرُنَا لَيْلًا
أَوْ نَهَارًا فَجَعَلْنَٰهَا حَصِيدًا كَأَن لَّمْ تَغْنَ بِٱلْأَمْسِ كَذَٰلِكَ نُفَصِّلُ
ٱلْءَايَٰتِ لِقَوْمٍ يَتَفَكَّرُونَ ﴿٢٤﴾ وَٱللَّهُ يَدْعُوٓا۟ إِلَىٰ دَارِ ٱلسَّلَٰمِ وَيَهْدِى مَن
يَشَآءُ إِلَىٰ صِرَٰطٍ مُّسْتَقِيمٍ ﴿٢٥﴾

The example of worldly life is just like the water We sent down from the sky, then the vegetation of the earth grew with it, which is (meant to be) eaten by men and cattle, until when the earth took on its ornament and was fully adorned, and its people thought that they had control over it, Our command came to it at night or by day, and We turned it into a stubble, as if it had not been there a day earlier. This is how We elaborate the signs for a people who reflect. And Allāh summons to the abode of peace, and leads whom He wills to a straight path. (Yūnus,10:24-25)

This life is temporary and to get a full appreciation of what that means, one only needs to look at the plants in one's backyard. How they sprout, grow to full vigor producing flowers, fruits and vegetables that please us, and then wilt and disappear. And sometimes, when it is Allāh's will, they may not even go through their normal lifecycle.

The real abode of peace and unmixed happiness is the Hereafter. And Qur'ān calls the humanity to that perfect bliss. The path leading to it is the Straight Path.

No Compulsion to Accept Islam

وَلَوْ شَآءَ رَبُّكَ لَآمَنَ مَن فِى ٱلْأَرْضِ كُلُّهُمْ جَمِيعًا ۚ أَفَأَنتَ تُكْرِهُ ٱلنَّاسَ
حَتَّىٰ يَكُونُوا۟ مُؤْمِنِينَ ﴿٩٩﴾

And if your Lord willed, all who are in the earth would have believed together. Would you compel men until they are believers? (Yūnus 10:99)

قُلْ يَـٰٓأَيُّهَا ٱلنَّاسُ قَدْ جَآءَكُمُ ٱلْحَقُّ مِن رَّبِّكُمْ ۖ فَمَنِ ٱهْتَدَىٰ
فَإِنَّمَا يَهْتَدِى لِنَفْسِهِۦ ۖ وَمَن ضَلَّ فَإِنَّمَا يَضِلُّ عَلَيْهَا ۖ وَمَآ أَنَا۠ عَلَيْكُم
بِوَكِيلٍ ﴿١٠٨﴾

Say: "O mankind! The truth from your Sustainer has now come unto you. Whoever, therefore, chooses to follow the right path, follows it but for his own good; and whoever chooses to go astray, goes but astray to his own hurt. And I am not responsible for your conduct." (Yūnus 10:108)

These two āyahs set it straight. We invite humanity to the Straight Path. Our job is only to deliver the message, not to compel or manipulate people into submission. Neither force nor fancy un-Islamic attractions or methods are to be used for this dawah mission because its purpose is not to win converts but to discharge our responsibility of delivering the message in its pure, unadulterated form.

Essential Qur'ānic Message

الٓر ۚ كِتَٰبٌ أُحْكِمَتْ ءَايَٰتُهُۥ ثُمَّ فُصِّلَتْ مِن لَّدُنْ حَكِيمٍ خَبِيرٍ ﴿١﴾ أَلَّا تَعْبُدُوٓا۟
إِلَّا ٱللَّهَ ۚ إِنَّنِى لَكُم مِّنْهُ نَذِيرٌ وَبَشِيرٌ ﴿٢﴾ وَأَنِ ٱسْتَغْفِرُوا۟ رَبَّكُمْ ثُمَّ تُوبُوٓا۟ إِلَيْهِ
يُمَتِّعْكُم مَّتَٰعًا حَسَنًا إِلَىٰٓ أَجَلٍ مُّسَمًّى وَيُؤْتِ كُلَّ ذِى فَضْلٍ فَضْلَهُۥ ۖ وَإِن
تَوَلَّوْا۟ فَإِنِّىٓ أَخَافُ عَلَيْكُمْ عَذَابَ يَوْمٍ كَبِيرٍ ﴿٣﴾ إِلَى ٱللَّهِ مَرْجِعُكُمْ ۖ وَهُوَ عَلَىٰ كُلِّ
شَىْءٍ قَدِيرٌ ﴿٤﴾

Alif , Lām , Rā . (This is) a book the āyahs of which have been made firm, and elaborated by the One who is All Wise, All Aware. (It teaches) that you should worship none but Allāh. (Say): "Verily I am (sent) unto you from Him to warn and to bring glad tidings. Ask your Sustainer to forgive you your sins, and then turn towards Him in repentance—(whereupon) He will grant you a goodly enjoyment of life (in this world) until a term set (by Him is fulfilled); and (in the life to come) He will bestow upon everyone possessed of merit (a full reward for) his merit. But if you turn away, then, verily, I dread for you the suffering (which is bound to befall you) on that awesome Day. To Allāh is your return, and He is powerful over everything." (Hūd 11:1-4)

The Qur'ān contains clear and firm guidance for the entire life. It comes from the All-Wise, All-Knowing Creator. It provides certain knowledge, not conjectures and speculations. The guidance covers our entire life, not just spiritual life, and promises total success. Those who follow it will also get a goodly enjoyment of this worldly life. Those who refuse to follow it stand to get the terrible punishment when they return to Allāh.

In essence the message is to realize the reality of the eternal life to come (*ākhirah*) and lead an *ākhirah* oriented life in this world.

We should also take note of the term مَّتَاعًا حَسَنًا (goodly enjoyment) used here to refer to the provisions of worldly life. Normally it is referred to as مَتَاعُ الْغُرُورِ (illusory enjoyment) in the Qur'ān. The difference tells us much about Islam's view of this world. When a person is occupied with the enjoyments and achievements of this world, with no concern for the Hereafter, this is an illusory enjoyment. When a person has his or her focus on the Hereafter (as called for here) and uses this life to prepare for that, then this same world becomes a goodly enjoyment.

Juz Twelve

Joys and Pains of this Life

وَلَئِنْ أَذَقْنَا ٱلْإِنسَـٰنَ مِنَّا رَحْمَةً ثُمَّ نَزَعْنَـٰهَا مِنْهُ إِنَّهُۥ لَيَـُٔوسٌ
كَفُورٌ ﴿٩﴾ وَلَئِنْ أَذَقْنَـٰهُ نَعْمَآءَ بَعْدَ ضَرَّآءَ مَسَّتْهُ لَيَقُولَنَّ
ذَهَبَ ٱلسَّيِّـَٔاتُ عَنِّىٓ ۚ إِنَّهُۥ لَفَرِحٌ فَخُورٌ ﴿١٠﴾ إِلَّا ٱلَّذِينَ صَبَرُوا۟ وَعَمِلُوا۟
ٱلصَّـٰلِحَـٰتِ أُو۟لَـٰٓئِكَ لَهُم مَّغْفِرَةٌ وَأَجْرٌ كَبِيرٌ ﴿١١﴾

And thus it is: if We let man taste some of Our grace, and then take it away from him—behold, he abandons all hope, forgetting all gratitude (for Our past favors). And thus it is: if We give him a taste of comfort after a hardship has touched him, he will say, "Evils have gone away from me", (and thus) He will become over-exulting, boastful. (And thus it is with most men—) save those who are patient in adversity and do righteous deeds: it is they whom forgiveness of sins awaits, and a great reward. (Hūd 11:9-11)

The big barrier to following an *ākhirah*-oriented life is the human weakness of being a slave to the present moment. Hardships in the now make us desperate; joys in the now make us exultant because we cannot see beyond the immediate. Patience and righteousness help us overcome this tendency and make us see the bigger picture of life, thereby promising forgiveness for our mistakes and great reward for our good deeds.

It may be noted that the pop culture and the consumerist society thrive on the desire for instant gratification. Marketing experts learn the art of exploiting this human weakness. And with the latest electronic gadgets, with their click-click and now tap-tap world, where results come in split seconds, this natural human weakness is taken to extremes. While we use them we need to take extra steps to counter these tendencies.

Pursuit of Happiness or Disaster

مَن كَانَ يُرِيدُ ٱلْحَيَوٰةَ ٱلدُّنْيَا وَزِينَتَهَا نُوَفِّ إِلَيْهِمْ أَعْمَٰلَهُمْ فِيهَا وَهُمْ فِيهَا
لَا يُبْخَسُونَ ﴿١٥﴾ أُو۟لَٰٓئِكَ ٱلَّذِينَ لَيْسَ لَهُمْ فِى ٱلْءَاخِرَةِ إِلَّا ٱلنَّارُ ۖ وَحَبِطَ
مَا صَنَعُوا۟ فِيهَا وَبَٰطِلٌ مَّا كَانُوا۟ يَعْمَلُونَ ﴿١٦﴾

Those who seek (merely) the worldly life and its beauty, We shall repay them in full for all that they did in this (life), and they shall not be deprived of their just due therein. It is they who, in the life to come, shall have nothing but the fire—for in vain shall be all that they wrought in this (world), and worthless all that they ever did! (Hūd 11:15-16)

This is again a very powerful reminder that a life led based on the idea that this world is all there is to it is entirely wasted. Good deeds performed without faith and without expectation of reward in the Hereafter are rewarded in this world. Such a person may get luxuries of this life and fame here, but nothing but disaster in the eternal life. Having the right motives and intentions is so important even for the apparently good deeds!

Response to Those Who Mock Our Religion

وَيَصْنَعُ ٱلْفُلْكَ وَكُلَّمَا مَرَّ عَلَيْهِ مَلَأٌ مِّن قَوْمِهِۦ سَخِرُوا۟ مِنْهُ ۚ قَالَ إِن تَسْخَرُوا۟ مِنَّا فَإِنَّا نَسْخَرُ مِنكُمْ كَمَا تَسْخَرُونَ ﴿٣٨﴾

He started making the Ark. Whenever the chieftains of his people passed by him, they scoffed at him. (Thereupon) he said: "If you are scoffing at us—behold, we are scoffing at you (and your ignorance), just as you are scoffing at us. (Hūd 11:38)

There is great support and inspiration here for those struggling to swim against the popular currents. As they know too well, the most visible symbols of an Islamic life are generally also the favorite targets of this popular pressure. Thus we see that in many Muslim countries even such a simple act as growing a beard (or observing hijab for women) are treated as crimes punishable by public ridicule! To go beyond that and challenge any of the established un-Islamic practices qualifies one to be labeled as a fanatic!

This episode from the story of Prophet Nūḥ عليه السلام is so telling. His final act of building the ark was considered proof positive by his people of he being out of his mind. Building a ship in an area nearly a thousand miles away from the sea! What could be crazier than that! They were having a great time, making fun of Prophet Nūḥ عليه السلام. Little did they realize that soon the Flood would wash away all of their ignorant self-assurance. One can imagine their horror when the end finally came, for it must have been in proportion to their delusion till that point.

We must realize that the most ridiculous thing would be for anyone to leave the Straight Path for fear of being ridiculed by those who are happily rushing on their path to eternal doom. The most laughable act is to trade truth for falsehood for fear of being laughed at. The craziest deed would be to knowingly disobey Allāh for fear of being called crazy!

Supporting Oppression

وَلَا تَرْكَنُوٓا۟ إِلَى ٱلَّذِينَ ظَلَمُوا۟ فَتَمَسَّكُمُ ٱلنَّارُ وَمَا لَكُم مِّن دُونِ ٱللَّهِ مِنْ أَوْلِيَآءَ ثُمَّ لَا تُنصَرُونَ ﴿١١٣﴾

And do not incline towards those who are bent on evildoing lest the fire (of the Hereafter) touch you: for (then) you would have none to protect you from Allāh, nor would you ever be helped (by Him). (Hūd 11:113)

There is a stern warning here that we should never lend any support to the powers of oppression and injustice. What is prohibited here is even a slight inclination towards them. Can we imagine the dire results for the oppressors themselves?

Good Deeds Drive Away Bad Deeds

وَأَقِمِ ٱلصَّلَوٰةَ طَرَفَىِ ٱلنَّهَارِ وَزُلَفًا مِّنَ ٱلَّيْلِ ۚ إِنَّ ٱلْحَسَنَـٰتِ يُذْهِبْنَ ٱلسَّيِّـَٔاتِ ۚ ذَٰلِكَ ذِكْرَىٰ لِلذَّٰكِرِينَ ﴿١١٤﴾

Establish Ṣalāh at both ends of the day, and in the early hours of the night. Surely, good deeds erase bad deeds. That is a reminder for the mindful. (Hūd 11:114)

This āyah covers the five daily obligatory ṣalāhs, details of which are in hadith. The five ṣalāhs set the rhythm of the daily life of a Muslim. They also act as strategically placed filters that sift out the dirt and contamination picked up during the course of the day to clean out a person's account of deeds.

The principle stated in the second part (good deeds drive away bad deeds) is a general one and we are asked to remember to always do some virtuous act after having committed a mistake, to wipe it out, although ṣalāh is especially emphasized for this purpose. If we make a mistake then as soon as we realize it, we should pull out the eraser and erase it. The mechanism works in three ways. 1) Good deeds cause the bad deeds to be erased from our record.[1] 2) They strike at one's inclination for doing bad deeds, thereby reducing the possibility of their recurrence. 3) They help create an environment for the community in which virtue flourishes and vice is curbed. However as Shāh ʿAbdul Qādir noted, the volume of good deeds is important to attain the desired results: The detergent should be in proportion to the laundry load.

Destruction of Nations

وَمَا كَانَ رَبُّكَ لِيُهْلِكَ ٱلْقُرَىٰ بِظُلْمٍ وَأَهْلُهَا مُصْلِحُونَ ﴿١١٧﴾

Your Lord is not such that He would destroy the towns unjustly, while as yet their people were putting things right. (Hūd 11:117)

This should set our perspective right on the causes of and way out from the destruction going on around the world. A nation would not be destroyed if it is engaged in reform. But

1 It should be noted that this wiping out of the sins by performing virtuous acts is limited to minor sins. Major sins require repentance and making retribution for their forgiveness. But the practice of performing a virtuous act after any sin is nevertheless valuable for the next two reasons mentioned above..

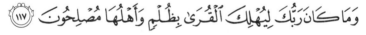

it is a candidate for punishment when evil and corruption becomes dominant in it and voices and efforts for reform have been marginalized.

Juz Thirteen

Sūrah Yūsuf

Sūrah Yūsuf is unique among Qur'ānic narratives as the entire sūrah is devoted to the story of Prophet Yūsuf ﵇. Further, his story, unlike other stories, is not mentioned anywhere else. The sūrah is filled with moral lessons, for which a good tafsīr should be consulted. Here are only some of those lessons.

In-between Muslims

ٱقْتُلُوا۟ يُوسُفَ أَوِ ٱطْرَحُوهُ أَرْضًا يَخْلُ لَكُمْ وَجْهُ أَبِيكُمْ وَتَكُونُوا۟ مِنۢ بَعْدِهِۦ قَوْمًا صَٰلِحِينَ ﴿٩﴾

"Let us kill Yūsuf, or throw him at some place on earth, and thus your father's full attention will be devoted for you alone, and after doing that, you may become a righteous people." (Yūsuf, 12:9)

The brothers of Prophet Yūsuf ﵇ were Muslims. They were driven by jealousy and not by an ideological conflict. But this jealousy led them to commit serious wrongs. Torn between their negative emotions and their sense of right and wrong, they were the in-between Muslims. They must have felt the pricks of conscience in formulating their evil plan. This is how they assuaged their guilt feeling. "Do this one wrong now, and afterward lead a virtuous life."

Anyone resorting to the same justification for any wrong should realize the hollowness of this logic.

Human Nature

This sūrah gives extremely valuable insights into human nature. It also tears apart the idea that good people are above lusts and desires or that there can be such a thing as platonic love. This idea only helps remove the safeguards thereby making succumbing to those desires easier.

This is the story of a Prophet, whose innocence is attested to by the Qur'ān. Yet it also says clearly that he could have succumbed to the lust, except for the help from Allāh. The following āyahs make it very clear.

وَلَقَدْ هَمَّتْ بِهِۦ ۖ وَهَمَّ بِهَا لَوْلَآ أَن رَّءَا بُرْهَـٰنَ رَبِّهِۦ ۚ كَذَٰلِكَ
لِنَصْرِفَ عَنْهُ ٱلسُّوٓءَ وَٱلْفَحْشَآءَ ۚ إِنَّهُۥ مِنْ عِبَادِنَا ٱلْمُخْلَصِينَ ﴿٢٤﴾

She certainly desired him, and he might have desired her, had he not seen the proof from his Lord. Thus We did, to turn evil and lewdness away from him. Surely, he was one of Our chosen servants. (Yūsuf, 12:24)

قَالَ رَبِّ ٱلسِّجْنُ أَحَبُّ إِلَىَّ مِمَّا يَدْعُونَنِىٓ إِلَيْهِ ۖ وَإِلَّا تَصْرِفْ عَنِّى كَيْدَهُنَّ
أَصْبُ إِلَيْهِنَّ وَأَكُن مِّنَ ٱلْجَـٰهِلِينَ ﴿٣٣﴾

He (Yūsuf) said, "My Lord, the prison is dearer to me than what these women invite me to do. If You do not turn their guile away from me, I might yet yield to their allure and become one of those who are unaware (of right and wrong). (Yūsuf, 12:33)

وَمَآ أُبَرِّئُ نَفْسِىٓ ۚ إِنَّ ٱلنَّفْسَ لَأَمَّارَةٌۢ بِٱلسُّوٓءِ إِلَّا مَا رَحِمَ رَبِّىٓ ۚ إِنَّ رَبِّى
غَفُورٌ رَّحِيمٌ ﴿٥٣﴾

And yet, I am not trying to absolve myself: for, verily, man's inner self does incite (him) to evil, and saved are only they upon whom my Sustainer bestows His grace. Certainly, my Sustainer is the Most-Forgiving, Very-Merciful. (Yūsuf 12:53)

In the first āyah Allāh is saying that Prophet Yūsuf عليه السلام might have desired her. In the second āyah Prophet Yūsuf عليه السلام is seeking Allāh's help against their seduction since without that help he might yield to their allure. The third āyah is a general observation about human nature which has inclinations to evil.

The idea that human beings can be reformed against their nature is a fantastic one. This story should liberate us from such illusions. The proper moral reform consists in recognizing human nature and eliminating the opportunities for it taking the wrong course. The attraction between the sexes is an important force of nature, which makes family life possible, which is the basic unit of society. When it spills outside marriage, it becomes a destructive force, which must be curbed. And the way to do that is to restrict the exposure and opportunities for interaction between the sexes in those situations. Hence the laws of hijab and the restrictions against free-mixing, which are based on a perfect knowledge of the human nature. All those who try to water them down are working against the forces of nature.

It should also be noted that Zulaykha was older than Prophet Yūsuf عليه السلام. He had entered their house as a child to be possibly adopted as a son. This removes any grounds for relaxation of the requirements of hijab for an *older* (as opposed to an old) woman. As long as the two are of marriageable age, the restrictions are to be observed.

Sermon in the Prison

إِنِّي تَرَكْتُ مِلَّةَ قَوْمٍ لَّا يُؤْمِنُونَ بِٱللَّهِ وَهُم بِٱلْـَٔاخِرَةِ هُمْ كَٰفِرُونَ ﴿٣٧﴾
وَٱتَّبَعْتُ مِلَّةَ ءَابَآءِيٓ إِبْرَٰهِيمَ وَإِسْحَٰقَ وَيَعْقُوبَۚ مَا كَانَ لَنَآ أَن نُّشْرِكَ
بِٱللَّهِ مِن شَيْءٍۚ ذَٰلِكَ مِن فَضْلِ ٱللَّهِ عَلَيْنَا وَعَلَى ٱلنَّاسِ وَلَٰكِنَّ أَكْثَرَ
ٱلنَّاسِ لَا يَشْكُرُونَ ﴿٣٨﴾ يَٰصَٰحِبَيِ ٱلسِّجْنِ ءَأَرْبَابٌ مُّتَفَرِّقُونَ
خَيْرٌ أَمِ ٱللَّهُ ٱلْوَٰحِدُ ٱلْقَهَّارُ ﴿٣٩﴾ مَا تَعْبُدُونَ مِن دُونِهِۦٓ إِلَّآ أَسْمَآءً
سَمَّيْتُمُوهَآ أَنتُمْ وَءَابَآؤُكُم مَّآ أَنزَلَ ٱللَّهُ بِهَا مِن سُلْطَٰنٍۚ إِنِ ٱلْحُكْمُ
إِلَّا لِلَّهِۚ أَمَرَ أَلَّا تَعْبُدُوٓاْ إِلَّآ إِيَّاهُۚ ذَٰلِكَ ٱلدِّينُ ٱلْقَيِّمُ وَلَٰكِنَّ أَكْثَرَ ٱلنَّاسِ
لَا يَعْلَمُونَ ﴿٤٠﴾

I have abandoned the way of those who do not believe in Allāh, and who are deniers of the Hereafter. And I follow the creed of my forefathers Ibrāhīm (Abraham), Isḥāq (Isaac), and Ya'qūb (Jacob). It is not conceivable that we should (be allowed to) ascribe divinity to anyone beside Allāh: this is (an outcome) of Allāh's bounty unto us and unto all mankind – but most people are ungrateful. O my companions in imprisonment! Which is more reasonable: (belief in the existence of numerous divine) lords, each of them different from the other—or (in) Allāh, the One God, who holds absolute sway over all that exists? All that you worship instead of Allāh is nothing but (empty) names which you have invented—you and your forefathers—(and) for which Allāh has bestowed no warrant from on high. Sovereignty belongs to none but Allāh. He has ordained that you shall not worship anyone but Him. This is the only right path. But most of the people do not know. (Yūsuf 12:37-40)

This is a very powerful sermon that passionately appeals to our ingrained sense of truth and falsehood to show the truth of the universal call of Islam. Prophet Yūsuf عليه السلام, like all prophets, is constantly on the lookout to call people to Allāh. He gets an opportunity when the inmates approach him for interpretation of their dreams. With great wisdom and passion he uses the occasion to deliver them the message. It is a penetrating question, which can be posed to all the polytheists of the world: "Which is more reasonable: (belief in the existence of numerous divine) lords, each of them different from the other—or (in) Allāh, the One God, who holds absolute sway over all that exists?"

It is telling that this important part of the story is completely missing from the narrative in the Torah, which otherwise has many historical details (names, places, numbers) not mentioned in the Qur'ān. Such details are a characteristic of human story telling. On the other hand the Qur'ān ignores such details and focuses totally on telling the stories to highlight the guidance for humanity inherent in them.

Tawakkul

وَقَالَ يَٰبَنِيَّ لَا تَدۡخُلُواْ مِنۢ بَابٖ وَٰحِدٖ وَٱدۡخُلُواْ مِنۡ أَبۡوَٰبٖ مُّتَفَرِّقَةٖۖ وَمَآ
أُغۡنِي عَنكُم مِّنَ ٱللَّهِ مِن شَيۡءٍۖ إِنِ ٱلۡحُكۡمُ إِلَّا لِلَّهِۖ عَلَيۡهِ تَوَكَّلۡتُۖ وَعَلَيۡهِ
فَلۡيَتَوَكَّلِ ٱلۡمُتَوَكِّلُونَ ٦٧

And he said, "O my sons, do not enter (the city) all of you from the same gate; rather, enter from different gates. And I cannot help you in any way against (the will of) Allāh. Sovereignty belongs to none but Allāh. In Him I place my trust, and all those who trust should trust in Him alone." (Yūsuf, 12:67)

For security reasons Prophet Yaʿqūb (Jacob) عليه السلام asked his sons not to travel together. But after advising them of the necessary precaution, he made it very clear that his trust was not in his prudence but in Allāh. This is a lesson in the very important concept of *tawakkul*: We should take the best steps needed based on our knowledge and understanding, then leave the results to Allāh. *Tawakkul* means making and executing the plans to the best of our ability and then putting our trust in Allāh to make our plans and actions bring out the desired outcomes. This is Islam's middle way between the extremes of taking matters completely in our hands or leaving them altogether and hoping for desired outcomes without any effort. *Tawakkul* ends worries and anxieties without compromising on our plans and actions.

Forgiveness

قَالَ لَا تَثْرِيبَ عَلَيْكُمُ ٱلْيَوْمَ ۖ يَغْفِرُ ٱللَّهُ لَكُمْ ۖ وَهُوَ أَرْحَمُ ٱلرَّٰحِمِينَ ﴿٩٢﴾

He said, "No reproach upon you today! May Allāh forgive you, and He is the Most- Merciful of all those who show mercy. (Yūsuf, 12:92)

وَقَدْ أَحْسَنَ بِىٓ إِذْ أَخْرَجَنِى مِنَ ٱلسِّجْنِ وَجَآءَ بِكُم مِّنَ ٱلْبَدْوِ مِنۢ بَعْدِ أَن نَّزَغَ ٱلشَّيْطَٰنُ بَيْنِى وَبَيْنَ إِخْوَتِىٓ

(My Lord) favored me when he released me from the prison, and brought you from the countryside after Satan had caused a rift between me and my brothers. (Yūsuf, 12:100)

This is the greatness of the Prophetic character, an example in both forgiveness and thankfulness. After all the ordeals through which his brothers had put him as a young child, he forgave them. And the forgiveness referred to in the first āyah mentioned above was really meant as we can see in the second āyah quoted above. Prophet Yūsuf عليه السلام, instead of blaming his brothers, simply referred to whatever happened to the inspirations of Satan.

When Prophet Muḥammad ﷺ conquered Makkah and he was in a position to take revenge from the Quraysh leaders who had left no stone unturned in hurting him and his followers for more than a decade, he used the same words to forgive them.

Prophet Yūsuf عليه السلام had faced three great tribulations. First, he was mistreated by his brothers. Second, he had to withstand long separation from his parents. Third, he was unjustly put in prison. Here in summing up his story he is giving a profound lesson in thankfulness. First, he reversed the order making the last incident the most important and the first, which had started it all and for which his brothers were directly responsible, the least. Second, he focused not on the ordeal but on the ending of the ordeal. He thanked Allāh for helping him get out of the prison, and for bringing back his parents and family. No complaints about his long ordeal, no ill feeling about his brothers. Only thanks and rejoicing.

Knowledge, Wisdom, Blindness

أَفَمَن يَعْلَمُ أَنَّمَآ أُنزِلَ إِلَيْكَ مِن رَّبِّكَ ٱلْحَقُّ كَمَنْ هُوَ أَعْمَىٰٓ ۚ إِنَّمَا يَتَذَكَّرُ أُو۟لُوا۟ ٱلْأَلْبَٰبِ ﴿١٩﴾

Now, can the one who knows that whatever has been revealed to you from your Lord is the truth, be equal to one who is blind? But only men of understanding heed. (Ar-Raʿd, 13:19)

Allāh's guidance has been mentioned in many places as the light. This light makes the believers see the truth as truth. Others are in utter darkness and therefore they cannot see it. That is, they are blind to it.

Worldly Provisions

ٱللَّهُ يَبْسُطُ ٱلرِّزْقَ لِمَن يَشَآءُ وَيَقْدِرُ ۚ وَفَرِحُوا۟ بِٱلْحَيَوٰةِ ٱلدُّنْيَا وَمَا ٱلْحَيَوٰةُ ٱلدُّنْيَا فِى
ٱلْءَاخِرَةِ إِلَّا مَتَٰعٌ ﴿٢٦﴾

Allāh expands the provision for whom He wills and narrows it (for whom He wills). And they (who are given abundance) rejoice in the life of this world—even though, as compared with the life to come, the life of this world is nothing but a fleeting pleasure. (Ar-Raʿd, 13:26)

Too many people get deceived into thinking that their economic achievements are a result of their own smarts. This āyah should help destroy this myth. A person who truly believes in this statement will always be thankful to Allāh for all his provisions and earnings, will not be tempted by ḥarām sources of income, and will be a contented person.

Peace of Mind

ٱلَّذِينَ ءَامَنُوا۟ وَتَطْمَئِنُّ قُلُوبُهُم بِذِكْرِ ٱللَّهِ ۗ أَلَا بِذِكْرِ ٱللَّهِ تَطْمَئِنُّ
ٱلْقُلُوبُ ﴿٢٨﴾

The ones who believe and their hearts are peaceful with the remembrance of Allāh. Listen, the hearts find peace only in the remembrance of Allāh. (Ar-Raʿd, 13:28)

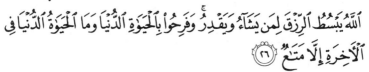

This is the real recipe for achieving that elusive peace of mind. Remembrance of Allāh (dhikr) brings one closer to Allāh. And as one gets closer to Allāh his worries and anxieties are replaced by tranquility and contentment.

Dhikr is the food for the soul. Nothing else would satisfy a healthy soul. On the other hand a sick soul may not be able to digest it, but it will find nothing else either that can provide proper nourishment for it. That is why the āyah first says that the guidance of Allāh is for those whose hearts find peace in the remembrance of Allāh. In other words those who have healthy souls. Then it tells that real peace lies only in the remembrance of Allāh.

Conquering Nature?

ٱللَّهُ ٱلَّذِى خَلَقَ ٱلسَّمَـٰوَٰتِ وَٱلْأَرْضَ وَأَنزَلَ مِنَ ٱلسَّمَآءِ مَآءً
فَأَخْرَجَ بِهِۦ مِنَ ٱلثَّمَرَٰتِ رِزْقًا لَّكُمْ ۖ وَسَخَّرَ لَكُمُ ٱلْفُلْكَ لِتَجْرِىَ
فِى ٱلْبَحْرِ بِأَمْرِهِۦ ۖ وَسَخَّرَ لَكُمُ ٱلْأَنْهَـٰرَ ﴿٣٢﴾ وَسَخَّرَ لَكُمُ ٱلشَّمْسَ
وَٱلْقَمَرَ دَآئِبَيْنِ ۖ وَسَخَّرَ لَكُمُ ٱلَّيْلَ وَٱلنَّهَارَ ﴿٣٣﴾

It is Allāh Who has created the heavens and the earth and sends down rain from the skies, and with it brings out fruits wherewith to feed you; it is He Who has made the ships subject to you, that they may sail through the sea by His command; and the rivers (also) has He made subject to you. And He has made subject to you the sun and the moon, both diligently pursuing their courses; and the night and the day has He (also) made subject to you. (Ibrāhīm 14:32-33)

Here is the cure for the delusion of modern science that it is conquering nature. We constantly hear how man has conquered the earth and is now out to conquer space. The apparent control over rivers and seas, mountains and deserts, and plants and animals that mankind seems to exert, the astounding ability with which the powers of the sun and the moon have been harnessed to serve human needs, the wonderful inventions that seem to put gigantic forces of nature at our disposal-all of these result from His Will. It is Allāh who created the universe and it is He who has granted us control over it. (And whenever He wills, He takes it back as well.) Instead of congratulating ourselves for "conquering" it, we should be thanking Allāh for granting us this domination.

The disasters that modern science has produced, especially the environmental disaster, are a result of its delusion. A scientist informed by this āyah will be freed from this debilitating sickness that is threatening the humanity. He would act responsibly, knowing that he is accountable before Allāh for how he uses the domination given to him as a test. He would be a grateful and humble servant of Allāh instead of the mad scientist out to maximize his power and profits. He would know that Allāh created the universe to serve us and created us to serve Him.

Juz Fourteen

Message of Sūrah al-Ḥijr

Sūrah al-Ḥijr was revealed in the early Makkan period. In fact it contains the āyah that ordered the beginning of public call to Islam. (Al-Ḥijr, 15:94). It contains stories of the nations of previous prophets. These nations refused to accept the call of the prophets and were destroyed. Stories of Prophets Ibrāhīm, Lūṭ, Shuʿayb, and Ṣāliḥ عليهم السلام are mentioned. The sūrah ends with two important commands.

A) Ignore the riches of the world

لَا تَمُدَّنَّ عَيْنَيْكَ إِلَىٰ مَا مَتَّعْنَا بِهِۦٓ أَزْوَٰجًا مِّنْهُمْ وَلَا تَحْزَنْ عَلَيْهِمْ وَٱخْفِضْ جَنَاحَكَ لِلْمُؤْمِنِينَ ﴿٨٨﴾

(So) turn not your eyes (longingly) towards the worldly benefits which We have granted unto some of those (that deny the truth), and neither grieve over those (who refuse to heed you), but spread the wings of your tenderness over the believers. (Al-Ḥijr 15:88)

The riches of this world can become a barrier to accepting and following the truth. They are a distraction that could cause a believer to stray from the Straight Path. While we do seek Allāh's blessings in worldly provisions, we should never look at the worldly possessions of others with envy. This āyah is the strongest antidote to the rat race.

B) Stay the course until the last minute

وَٱعْبُدْ رَبَّكَ حَتَّىٰ يَأْتِيَكَ ٱلْيَقِينُ ﴿٩٩﴾

And serve your Lord till the Inevitable (death) comes unto you. (Al-Ḥijr 15:99)

Our commitment to submit to Allāh should not be a fad, a temporary emotional reaction, or a seasonal act (like only in Ramadan). It is a lifelong devotion from which we should not waver despite all the highs and lows of life. The goal is to reach the end of our life in a state of total submission to our Creator.

Humble Biological Beginnings

خَلَقَ ٱلْإِنسَٰنَ مِن نُّطْفَةٍ فَإِذَا هُوَ خَصِيمٌ مُّبِينٌ ﴿٤﴾

He has created man from a sperm-drop; and behold this same (man) becomes an open disputer! (An-Naḥl, 16:4)

In many places in the Qur'ān we are reminded of our very humble biological beginnings as a check on the tendency to rationalize and philosophize our refusal to obey the commands of our Creator. Remembering how our own life started may give us the perspective so we do not get carried away with our superficial academic arguments. Just visualize a drop of semen arguing with the Creator of the universe.

How Allāh Creates

إِنَّمَا قَوْلُنَا لِشَيْءٍ إِذَآ أَرَدْنَٰهُ أَن نَّقُولَ لَهُۥ كُن فَيَكُونُ ﴿٤٠﴾

Whenever We will anything to be, We but say unto it Our word "Be"—and it is. (An-Naḥl, 16:40)

Allāh created this world out of nothing. How? Through His command: Be, and it was. The resurrection will be the same way. There is absolutely nothing to stop Allāh's Will from coming into reality. It occurs precisely when and how He decides it to take place.

A very powerful Hadith Qudsī[1] says it so beautifully: "Allāh says: O My Slaves! All of you are lost except those whom I guide. So ask Me for guidance, I will guide you. And all of you are poor save those whom I enrich. So ask Me, I will give you. All of you are sinners except those whom I save. So he who seeks forgiveness from Me knowing that I am the one with the power to forgive, I will forgive him and it does not bother Me (how many I forgive).

And if your first and your last, your living and your dead, your youthful and your exhausted, gather together to have hearts as the heart of the most righteous of My slaves that will not increase My domain by even so much as the wing of a mosquito.

And if your first and your last, your living and your dead, your youthful and your exhausted gather together to have hearts as the heart of the most wretched of My slaves that will

1 A Hadith Qudsī is a hadith in which the Prophet ﷺ quotes a saying of Allāh.

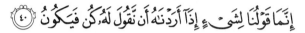

not diminish My kingdom by even so much as the wing of a mosquito.

And if your first and your last, your living and your dead, your youthful and your exhausted gather together on one ground and each one of you prays to Me for all his desires and I give everyone what they are asking for that will not diminish from My kingdom except as much as the water withdrawn from the ocean if you were to immerse a needle in it.

This is because I am Jawwād (the Bountiful) and Mājid (the Glorious). I do what I will. My grant is a word and my punishment is a word. My only command to anything when I intend it is that I say to it "Be" and it is."[2]

Asking those Who Know

وَمَآ أَرۡسَلۡنَا مِن قَبۡلِكَ إِلَّا رِجَالٗا نُّوحِيٓ إِلَيۡهِمۡۚ فَسۡـَٔلُوٓاْ أَهۡلَ ٱلذِّكۡرِ إِن كُنتُمۡ لَا تَعۡلَمُونَ ﴿٤٣﴾

We did not send (messengers) before you other than men whom We inspired with revelation. So, ask the people (having the knowledge) of the Reminder (the earlier Scriptures), if you do not know. (An-Naḥl, 16:43)

This āyah tells us that those who do not know should ask those who do. While the reason for this is so self-evident, it is amazing how many people insist on doing the opposite when it comes to religious knowledge.

Islam does not have a formal church like the Catholic Church for example. However it does not mean that everybody has equal knowledge, or equal right to offer religious opinions regardless of the state of their knowledge. Those who do not know should first acknowledge that they do not know and

2 Abū Dharr رضي الله عنه in *Sunan at-Tirmidhī*, ابواب صفة القيامة [Chapter: Description of the Day of Judgment, etc].

then should inquire from those who do. This principle is the basis for following the imams in matters of fiqh.

This āyah also informs us that all messengers were men. The essential human equality between the genders (see below) does not call for a negation of their different roles in life.

Right and Wrong: Most Comprehensive Āyah

إِنَّ ٱللَّهَ يَأْمُرُ بِٱلْعَدْلِ وَٱلْإِحْسَٰنِ وَإِيتَآيِٕ ذِى ٱلْقُرْبَىٰ وَيَنْهَىٰ
عَنِ ٱلْفَحْشَآءِ وَٱلْمُنكَرِ وَٱلْبَغْىِ ۚ يَعِظُكُمْ لَعَلَّكُمْ
تَذَكَّرُونَ ﴿٩٠﴾

Allāh enjoins justice and kindness, and giving to relatives (their due rights), and forbids lewdness and abomination and wickedness. He exhorts you so that you may take heed. (An-Naḥl, 16:90)

This āyah encapsulates the most important Islamic teachings and has been called the most comprehensive āyah dealing with right and wrong. Three things top the list of do's: Justice, good behavior, charity. Three top the list of don'ts: Obscenity, injustice, oppression. These teachings are so important to building the Islamic community that we must keep them in front of us all the time. That is why ʿUmar ibn ʿAbdul ʿAzīz, known generally as the fifth rightly guided khalīfah, and who was a great scholar in his own right, started the practice of including this āyah in the Jumuah khuṭbah. This wonderful practice continues to date.

ʿAdl means justice with friend and foe alike. This is the bedrock of Islamic polity. ʿAdl also implies *iʿtidāl* or following the middle path and avoiding all extremes. Needless to say it includes avoiding the extremes that are propagated in the name of moderation.

Iḥsān means going the extra mile. Giving people more than their due. This is what brings beauty and warmth in relationships. It also means acting with the consciousness that Allāh is watching. That would naturally bring out the best of us in every deed.

The third command deals with good family relations, which Islam has elevated to a very high level among virtues. That is why it has been separately mentioned here although it would be covered by the first two in a general way.

Faḥshā' covers all obscenities and acts of lewdness. This is everything that nurtures and excites lust. *Munkar* is a general term that refers to all those evils that sensible human nature would abhor, whether lying, cheating, exploiting others, or committing the acts that Allāh has declared as sins. It is the antonym of *maʿrūf* which literally means "well-known" and refers to acts known to be good by the Islamic community. *Baghy* refers to acts of oppression.

These three prohibitions cover the entire agenda for moral reform. As Sufi masters explain there are three faculties in human nature whose balance is the goal of self reform. These are desires, intellect, and anger. Thus of the three dont's mentioned here, the first deals with out-of-control cravings, the second with an intellect suppressed (by Satanic inspirations or otherwise), and the third with out-of-control anger.

Essential Equality between Men and Women

مَنْ عَمِلَ صَٰلِحًا مِّن ذَكَرٍ أَوْ أُنثَىٰ وَهُوَ مُؤْمِنٌ فَلَنُحْيِيَنَّهُۥ حَيَوٰةً
طَيِّبَةً ۖ وَلَنَجْزِيَنَّهُمْ أَجْرَهُم بِأَحْسَنِ مَا كَانُوا۟ يَعْمَلُونَ ﴿٩٧﴾

Whoever, male or female, has acted righteously, while being a believer, We shall certainly make him live a good life, and We shall bestow on such their reward according to the best of their actions. (An-Naḥl, 16:97)

Islam asserts that men and women have separate spheres for their endeavors in this life. But underlying this separateness is a basic moral and human equality. This is mentioned here. When each one of them performs the right deeds based on their station in life, they will get the reward of a pure, enjoyable, and rewarding life here and best recompense in the Hereafter, regardless of their gender.

Calling to Islam

ٱدْعُ إِلَىٰ سَبِيلِ رَبِّكَ بِٱلْحِكْمَةِ وَٱلْمَوْعِظَةِ ٱلْحَسَنَةِ ۖ وَجَٰدِلْهُم بِٱلَّتِي
هِيَ أَحْسَنُ ۚ إِنَّ رَبَّكَ هُوَ أَعْلَمُ بِمَن ضَلَّ عَن سَبِيلِهِۦ ۖ وَهُوَ أَعْلَمُ
بِٱلْمُهْتَدِينَ ﴿١٢٥﴾

Invite (people) to the way of your Sustainer with wisdom and good counsel. And argue with them in the best of manners. Surely, your Sustainer knows best the one who deviates from His way, and He knows best the ones who are on the right path. (An-Naḥl, 16:125)

This is the essential guidance for anyone engaged in calling others to Islam. We must call others to Islam with wisdom and using the best manners. Even when we have to enter a debate with the non-believers, it must be done in a most beautiful way. Ḥikmah (wisdom) implies, among other things, intellectual strength of the argument being presented.

Al-Mawʿidhat al-Ḥasanah implies speaking with sincerity, kindness, and compassion. The entire call to Islam should be such that any open minded person could realize that the caller is a well wisher who is driven by a sincere desire to help them and that the arguments he is presenting make sense. Further the caller to Islam should never be provoked into unseemly behavior by stubborn opponents. Stories of the Prophets in the Qurʾān illustrate all these points in action.

Juz Fifteen

This juz begins with Sūrah al-Isrā' (also known as Sūrah Banī Isrā'īl). The very first āyah establishes the permanent, irrevocable importance of Masjid al-Aqṣā for Muslims. It refers to the miraculous night journey of Prophet Muḥammad ﷺ from Makkah to Jerusalem and from there to the high heavens for a meeting with Allāh, Most High. The second part of this journey is known as Mi'rāj or Ascension. This second part is mentioned later in Sūrah an-Najm (53).

The five daily prayers were ordained during Mi'rāj and are referred to in āyah 78 in this sūrah.

This event took place toward the end of the Makkan period and signified the beginning of a new era where Islam would be established as a state. Thus important commandments for collective life were given in this sūrah in āyahs 22-39. The beginning and ending āyahs of this section are given below.

Tawḥīd

لَّا تَجْعَلْ مَعَ ٱللَّهِ إِلَٰهًا ءَاخَرَ فَتَقْعُدَ مَذْمُومًا مَّخْذُولًا ﴿٢٢﴾

Do not set up any other deity besides Allāh, otherwise you will find yourself disgraced and forsaken. (Al-Isrā', 17:22)

ذَٰلِكَ مِمَّآ أَوْحَىٰٓ إِلَيْكَ رَبُّكَ مِنَ ٱلْحِكْمَةِ ۗ وَلَا تَجْعَلْ مَعَ ٱللَّهِ إِلَٰهًا ءَاخَرَ فَتُلْقَىٰ
فِى جَهَنَّمَ مَلُومًا مَّدْحُورًا ﴿٣٩﴾

This is part of that knowledge of right and wrong which your Sustainer has revealed to you. Hence, do not set up any other deity besides Allāh, lest you be cast into hell, blamed (by yourself) and rejected (by Him)! (Al-Isrā', 17:39)

The list begins and ends with the reminder that we must not worship anyone except Allāh alone. Corrupt practices have corrupt ideas behind them and to remove the corruption from our lives, we must begin with the purification of our ideas and beliefs. Thus *tawḥīd* is the all important belief. A talk of "good deeds" is meaningless without it. *Tawḥīd* is the cornerstone of Islamic life, and *shirk* (polytheism) is its exact opposite. It follows that it must be a Muslim's top most concern to avoid *shirk* of all forms in his beliefs and practices.

Parental Rights

وَقَضَىٰ رَبُّكَ أَلَّا تَعْبُدُوٓا۟ إِلَّآ إِيَّاهُ وَبِٱلْوَٰلِدَيْنِ إِحْسَٰنًا ۚ إِمَّا يَبْلُغَنَّ عِندَكَ
ٱلْكِبَرَ أَحَدُهُمَآ أَوْ كِلَاهُمَا فَلَا تَقُل لَّهُمَآ أُفٍّ وَلَا تَنْهَرْهُمَا وَقُل

لَّهُمَا قَوۡلٗا كَرِيمٗا ٢٣ وَٱخۡفِضۡ لَهُمَا جَنَاحَ ٱلذُّلِّ مِنَ ٱلرَّحۡمَةِ
وَقُل رَّبِّ ٱرۡحَمۡهُمَا كَمَا رَبَّيَانِي صَغِيرٗا ٢٤

Your Sustainer has decreed that you worship none but Him, and do good unto your parents. If any one of them or both of them reach old age, do not say to them: *uff* (a word or expression of anger or disgust) and do not scold them, and address them with respectful words. And, out of kindness, lower to them the wing of humility, and say: "My Sustainer! Bestow on them your Mercy just as they cherished me in childhood." (Al-Isrā', 17:23-24)

These āyahs set the bar for kindness to parents so high that no one can ever be complacent about it and think that they have done all that they should have done. And to compensate for our shortcomings, we should be regularly praying for our parents as mentioned in the second āyah.

It should be kept in mind that parents have rights even when they are non-Muslims. In the hierarchy of rights, parental rights are the greatest among all the rights of other human beings. But they are subservient to the rights of Allāh. Thus one cannot revoke obedience to Allāh under the command of his or her parents. Although even in that situation politeness is required.

Being Spendthrift

وَءَاتِ ذَا ٱلۡقُرۡبَىٰ حَقَّهُۥ وَٱلۡمِسۡكِينَ وَٱبۡنَ ٱلسَّبِيلِ وَلَا تُبَذِّرۡ تَبۡذِيرًا
٢٦ إِنَّ ٱلۡمُبَذِّرِينَ كَانُوٓاْ إِخۡوَٰنَ ٱلشَّيَٰطِينِۖ وَكَانَ ٱلشَّيۡطَٰنُ لِرَبِّهِۦ
كَفُورٗا ٢٧

And render to the kindred their due rights, as (also) to those in want, and to the wayfarer: But squander not (your wealth) in the manner of a spendthrift. Verily spendthrifts are brothers of the satans; and the Satan is very ungrateful to his Sustainer. (Al-Isrā', 17:26-27)

There are two related terms used in the Qur'ān regarding improper spending. *Tabdhīr*, used here, is spending on projects for which no spending is justified. *Isrāf*, mentioned elsewhere, is spending extravagantly on projects which are in themselves permissible. Both are condemned. Unfortunately, both are very common in the Muslim world today. The extravagant spending in weddings and celebrations, so common today one might think that it was normal or fine, is just one example of this epidemic.

Killing Children for Fear of Poverty

وَلَا تَقْتُلُوٓاْ أَوْلَٰدَكُمْ خَشْيَةَ إِمْلَٰقٍ ۖ نَّحْنُ نَرْزُقُهُمْ وَإِيَّاكُمْ ۚ إِنَّ قَتْلَهُمْ كَانَ خِطْـًٔا كَبِيرًا ﴿٣١﴾

Do not kill your children for fear of poverty. We provide sustenance to them and to you, too. Killing them is a great sin indeed. (Al-Isrā', 17:31)

This also refers to abortions. While the āyah refers to the economic motive, as it was the common motive in pre-Islamic Jāhiliyyah, it is obvious that killing for other reasons is no more permissible. Birth control for fear of poverty, as a personal or national project, is also prohibited in Islam.

Adultery and Fornication

وَلَا تَقْرَبُوا۟ ٱلزِّنَىٰٓ ۖ إِنَّهُۥ كَانَ فَٰحِشَةً وَسَآءَ سَبِيلًا ﴿٣٢﴾

Do not even go close to fornication. It is indeed a shameful act, and an evil way to follow. (Al-Isrā', 17:32)

Islam does not just prohibit all extramarital sex, it also closes the doors that may lead to it. That is why what is prohibited here is getting close to fornication. This means it is obligatory to stay away from things that can excite the desires and situations that can make extramarital sex possible or easy. The problem today is that while societies *still* claim that they want to eliminate adultery, they insist on leaving open all the channels that lead to it. Their strategies make as much sense as putting a pot full of water on the stove and turning on the stove, then prohibiting the production of steam.

Today's media based commercial and cultural propaganda campaigns have put all their energy in exciting sexual desires because they help sell. The same can be said about the music industry, fashion industry, film industry, and all sorts of businesses that make money from exploitation of lust. This is the first time in history that the inviting picture of a woman has been placed on every square inch of available space. Coeducation and free mixing in general which have become commonplace today and are considered as marks of human progress, all stoke the fires that lead to fornication and adultery and all sorts of sexual perversions. The pot is full and the heat setting is at the highest level. Is it any wonder that steam production is also at the highest levels?

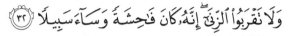

Quite expectedly those who have chosen to declare fueling the fires as a fundamental human right have taken fornication off the list of crimes. This makes the statistics not look as bad, but does not change anything in reality. The destruction of family life, which has reached epidemic proportions, is a direct result of this attitude.

Islam's call is to end this fatal contradiction and self delusion. Solve the problem at its roots. Close the doors that lead to sexual anarchy. It is a shame that the Muslim world, in large parts, has also become deaf to this Qur'ānic message with the result that the graphs of incidents of sexual crimes are at an all time high and going up. This is another reminder that our problems will not be solved until we start listening to the Qur'ān.

Murder

وَلَا تَقْتُلُوا۟ ٱلنَّفْسَ ٱلَّتِى حَرَّمَ ٱللَّهُ إِلَّا بِٱلْحَقِّ ۗ وَمَن قُتِلَ مَظْلُومًا فَقَدْ
جَعَلْنَا لِوَلِيِّهِۦ سُلْطَـٰنًا فَلَا يُسْرِف فِّى ٱلْقَتْلِ ۖ إِنَّهُۥ كَانَ مَنصُورًا ﴿٣٣﴾

And do not take any human being's life—(the life) which Allāh has willed to be sacred—otherwise than in (the pursuit of) justice. Hence, if anyone has been slain wrongfully, We have empowered his heir (to exact a just retribution); but even so, let him not exceed the bounds of equity in (retributive) killing. Surely, he will be helped (in a just retribution). (Al-Isrā', 17:33)

Killing is permitted only in the execution of a legal sentence,in a just war, or in legitimate self-defense. The overriding concern for justice demands that we avoid excesses in both directions: in letting murderers go unpunished, or going beyond limits in punishing the murderer and even others merely suspected of capital crimes. We see both extremes in the world today. Murderers go unpunished as capital sentence is considered too harsh. Yet killing men, women, and children on mere suspicions using remote killing mechanisms (like drones) is considered legitimate, even virtuous.

Vain Pursuits

وَلَا تَقْفُ مَا لَيْسَ لَكَ بِهِۦ عِلْمٌ ۚ إِنَّ ٱلسَّمْعَ وَٱلْبَصَرَ وَٱلْفُؤَادَ كُلُّ أُو۟لَٰٓئِكَ
كَانَ عَنْهُ مَسْـُٔولًا ﴿٣٦﴾

And pursue not that of which you have no knowledge; verily, (your) hearing and sight and heart—all of them—will be called to account for it (on Judgment Day). (Al-Isrā', 17:36)

This is banning idle curiosities, vain pursuits, and all pointless uses of our faculties of sense and intellect. This is the stuff that fills up most of the modern media and countless hours in Internet surfing, chatting, and texting. Social networks have taken this human weakness to an entirely new plane.

This is a reminder that our use of our faculties must be made with a heavy sense of responsibility and accountability before Allāh. Only this sense of ultimate accountability can prevent us from misusing these God given faculties.

Arrogance

وَلَا تَمْشِ فِى ٱلْأَرْضِ مَرَحًا ۖ إِنَّكَ لَن تَخْرِقَ ٱلْأَرْضَ وَلَن تَبْلُغَ ٱلْجِبَالَ
طُولًا ﴿٣٧﴾

And walk not on earth with haughty self-conceit: for, verily, you can never rend the earth asunder, nor can you ever grow as tall as the mountains! (Al-Isrā', 17:37)

This is meant to cut the megalomaniacs of all grades to size. A six foot tall human being walking arrogantly on the face of this vast earth, in comparison to which he is nothing more than a speck, makes an interesting spectacle. Let us be honest—and be humble.

Juz Sixteen

Sūrah Al-Kahf

This sūrah starts in the fifteenth juz and is concluded in the sixteenth. It is highly recommended that we recite it every Friday. Several ahadith promise that those who do so will be protected from the deceptions of Dajjāl. The Dajjāl will be a person who personifies deception. His will be an era of extreme trials and tribulations for the believers. We are asked to always pray for protection against those trials. While the Dajjāl has not yet appeared, we are indeed living in an age when dajjālic deceptions are increasingly manifest all around us.[1]

The story of the People of the Cave is narrated in āyahs 9-26. These were young people for whom their faith was all important. They lived at a time when the people of faith were being persecuted by a ruthless king. They could not fight him, nor could they surrender to him. So they took refuge in a cave. They put their affair in the Hands of Allāh and He

---

1 For a fuller discussion of how the message of sūrah al-Kahf protects us from these deceptions, one may read Maulana Syed Abul Hasan Ali Nadwi's *Faith versus Materialism: The Message of Surat al-Al-Kahf.*

saved them from persecution through a miraculous sleep that lasted for three centuries.

The story of Prophet Mūsā عليه السلام and Khiḍr is narrated in āyahs 60-82. Its most important moral is that things are not always what they appear to be. We should not be deceived or disheartened by the events that unfold before us every day. What seems to be an imperfect world is actually a perfect testing ground.

The story of Dhul Qarnayn is told in āyahs 83-98. He was a powerful, just, and Allāh fearing king. Two actions of his are specially highlighted.

1) His declaration that he would punish the unjust and deal kindly with the virtuous. This makes moral purpose and virtue as the yardstick with which to measure any ruler. In contrast secular western democracy holds that the government has no business deciding morality or virtue.

2) He refused to tax the people for a national project even when the tax was offered by the people. This was obviously not for the purpose of improving his chances of reelection; it was the extension of morality and virtue to the economic field.

Here are reflections on some āyahs from this sūrah.

InshāAllāh

وَلَا تَقُولَنَّ لِشَاْىْءٍ إِنِّي فَاعِلٌ ذَٰلِكَ غَدًا ﴿٢٣﴾ إِلَّآ أَن يَشَآءَ ٱللَّهُ ۚ وَٱذْكُر رَّبَّكَ إِذَا نَسِيتَ

And never say about anything, "I shall surely do this tomorrow," without (adding), "If Allāh so wills." And remember your Lord if you forget. (Al-Kahf, 18:23-24).

Here is the background for this āyah. The account of the Seven Sleepers, the encounter between Prophet Mūsā ﵇ and Khiḍr, and the story of the king Dhul Qarnayn were unknown to the Arabs. The Quraysh of Makkah were advised by Jewish scholars in Madinah to ask the Prophet ﷺ about them as a test of the authenticity of his prophethood. He promised to answer the question the next day expecting the revelation to come by that time. This sūrah was the answer. (This was a most brilliant answer that not only gave details about them, but also applied their stories to the situation at hand to show that the Quraysh were on the side of wrong in the stories about right and wrong. Unfortunately obstinacy kept the Quraysh and the Jews from accepting the Truth.)

This sūrah was the answer, but it was delayed by two weeks. The two anxious weeks were a Divine reminder of an important message mentioned in this āyah. We should never announce plans about the future as if we control it. Rather we should qualify these by the words, inshāAllāh (If Allāh wills).

There was a time when in the Western world, the phrase God willing, carried the same message. Today the secularized discourse shies away from acknowledging that we do not control the future. And even when it does acknowledge that, it refuses to acknowledge that the control belongs to God. So "God willing" is replaced by any number of clumsy expressions, whose common concern is to avoid mentioning God, like "If fate decrees," "If the wind blows right," "Hope it's my lucky day," "Barring some unforeseen (circumstance/incident/accident)," "If things work out," and "If things go according to plan." Superstition also reigns supreme as people normally say "knock on wood" or "keep your fingers crossed."

We should not give in to this secular madness. We need to bring inshāAllāh[2] (and God willing) back to our everyday discourse—on every continent and in every language of the world. For wherever we are and whatever language we speak, the future is always totally in the Hands of Allāh.

Extremism

وَٱصْبِرْ نَفْسَكَ مَعَ ٱلَّذِينَ يَدْعُونَ رَبَّهُم بِٱلْغَدَوٰةِ وَٱلْعَشِىِّ يُرِيدُونَ
وَجْهَهُۥ ۖ وَلَا تَعْدُ عَيْنَاكَ عَنْهُمْ تُرِيدُ زِينَةَ ٱلْحَيَوٰةِ ٱلدُّنْيَا ۖ وَلَا تُطِعْ مَنْ
أَغْفَلْنَا قَلْبَهُۥ عَن ذِكْرِنَا وَٱتَّبَعَ هَوَىٰهُ وَكَانَ أَمْرُهُۥ فُرُطًا ﴿٢٨﴾

Keep yourself content with those who call their Sustainer morning and evening, seeking His countenance, and let not your eyes overlook them, seeking the splendor of the worldly life. And do not obey the one whose heart We have made heedless of Our remembrance, and who has followed his desire and whose behavior has exceeded the limits. (Al-Kahf, 18:28)

Here is the most profound—and ignored—truth about extremism. Those who do not remember Allāh end up following their own desires and go to extremes in satisfying them. It all starts from a single minded devotion to the splendor of this worldly life. Extremism is thus a direct and inevitable result of materialism and unbelief. And turning to Allāh—and away from obedience to our lusts and greed—is the only way to fight it.

2 Recently the spelling of this expression has received undue attention due to some misconceptions about the meaning of the phrase when "inshā" is written together in English (as opposed to "in shā"). The fact is that readers of English tend to pronounce and understand it in the same manner when written as "inshallāh" or "inshāAllāh» or «in shaa Allāh.» In all cases they clearly understand it to mean «If Allāh wills.» So all are valid forms as affirmed by many scholars.

The Life of this World

وَٱضْرِبْ لَهُم مَّثَلَ ٱلْحَيَوٰةِ ٱلدُّنْيَا كَمَآءٍ أَنزَلْنَٰهُ مِنَ ٱلسَّمَآءِ فَٱخْتَلَطَ
بِهِۦ نَبَاتُ ٱلْأَرْضِ فَأَصْبَحَ هَشِيمًا تَذْرُوهُ ٱلرِّيَٰحُ ۗ وَكَانَ ٱللَّهُ عَلَىٰ كُلِّ شَىْءٍ
مُّقْتَدِرًا ﴿٤٥﴾

Set forth to them the similitude of the life of this world: It is like the rain which we send down from the skies: the earth's vegetation absorbs it, but soon it becomes dry stubble, which the winds do scatter: it is (only) Allāh who prevails over all things. (Al-Kahf, 18:45)

All the pleasures and riches of this world are short-lived. Here today, gone tomorrow. How foolish that one should make them the yardstick to measure success in life. This comment follows the account of the encounter of two characters: a rich non-believer and a poor believer. The latter was not at all impressed by the riches of the former and was much concerned about his unbelief and ungratefulness towards Allāh. The former refused to listen to him and was destroyed. This āyah captures the moral of the story.

That encounter continues today and so does the need for remembering the story and its moral.

The Greatest Loss

قُلْ هَلْ نُنَبِّئُكُم بِٱلْأَخْسَرِينَ أَعْمَٰلًا ﴿١٠٣﴾ ٱلَّذِينَ ضَلَّ سَعْيُهُمْ فِى ٱلْحَيَوٰةِ ٱلدُّنْيَا وَهُمْ
يَحْسَبُونَ أَنَّهُمْ يُحْسِنُونَ صُنْعًا ﴿١٠٤﴾ أُو۟لَٰٓئِكَ ٱلَّذِينَ كَفَرُوا۟ بِـَٔايَٰتِ رَبِّهِمْ وَلِقَآئِهِۦ
فَحَبِطَتْ أَعْمَٰلُهُمْ فَلَا نُقِيمُ لَهُمْ يَوْمَ ٱلْقِيَٰمَةِ وَزْنًا ﴿١٠٥﴾

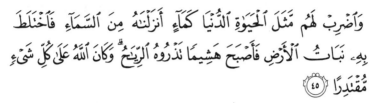

Say, "Shall We tell you about the greatest losers in respect of (their) deeds? Those are the ones whose effort in the worldly life has gone in vain, while they think they are doing well. Those are the ones who rejected the signs of their Sustainer and (the concept of) meeting with Him, so their deeds have gone to waste, and We shall assign to them no weight at all." (Al-Kahf, 18:103-105)

Good deeds without the right motives are a waste. Motives are the soul of every action. In turn motives are driven by belief. When belief in Allāh and the Hereafter is absent then one's good deeds are soulless.

This is an all important reminder that we need to purify both our intentions and our actions. If we do not seek rewards from Allāh in the Hereafter, we'll surely not get them.

The Blessed People

أُو۟لَٰٓئِكَ ٱلَّذِينَ أَنْعَمَ ٱللَّهُ عَلَيْهِم مِّنَ ٱلنَّبِيِّـۧنَ مِن ذُرِّيَّةِ ءَادَمَ وَمِمَّنْ حَمَلْنَا مَعَ
نُوحٍ وَمِن ذُرِّيَّةِ إِبْرَٰهِيمَ وَإِسْرَٰٓءِيلَ وَمِمَّنْ هَدَيْنَا وَٱجْتَبَيْنَآ ۚ إِذَا تُتْلَىٰ عَلَيْهِمْ ءَايَٰتُ
ٱلرَّحْمَٰنِ خَرُّوا۟ سُجَّدًا وَبُكِيًّا ۩ ﴿٥٨﴾

Those are the people on whom Allāh bestowed His grace, the prophets from the progeny of 'Ādam, and of those whom We caused to board (the Ark) along with Nūḥ, and from the progeny of Ibrāhīm and Isrā'īl (Jacob), and (all of them were) whom We guided and selected. When the āyahs of The Raḥmān (The All-Merciful) were recited before them, they used to fall down in Sajdah (prostration), while they were weeping. (Maryam, 19:58)

In sūrah al-Fātiḥah we make the dua to be shown the path of those on whom Allāh bestowed His grace. Here the same exact word is being used to tell us that the prophets were the people who were so favored. So anyone sincerely looking to find Allāh's true favors and blessings should be following in the footsteps of the prophets.

And the thing to note in their behavior is their attitude toward the words and commands of Allāh. Falling down in sajdah with tears of love and awe in their eyes captures their willing and loving devotion to Allāh and His commands.

We can judge where we stand with reference to Allāh's true blessings and grace, by seeing where we stand in relationship to Allāh's words and commands.

Reflections on Āyahs of Sajdah (Prostration)

This is one of the fourteen āyahs of sajdah in the Qur'ān. These āyahs are themselves a reminder of the miracle of the Qur'ān. When reciting any of these āyahs, or listening to their recitation, inside the ṣalāh or outside, believers always perform sajdah. That simple act of prostration that we do not think much of is in reality an extraordinary event. To realize that we can ask if anyone can produce a book such that whenever readers reach a certain point in it they will perform a prescribed act of devotion. All of them. All the time. We can challenge the multibillion dollar publishing empires to pool all their resources and marketing talents to produce such a book. They will fail. For only the Words of Allāh can command such devotion.

There is another important message here. We cannot approach the Qur'ān as another book, to be critically evaluated and judged and selectively accepted or rejected based on one's understanding. This is the way an Orientalist will approach the Qur'ān. But for a Muslim these āyahs set the tone for all our interaction with it; it is one of total and loving submission.

Importance of Ṣalāh

فَخَلَفَ مِنۢ بَعۡدِهِمۡ خَلۡفٌ أَضَاعُواْ ٱلصَّلَوٰةَ وَٱتَّبَعُواْ ٱلشَّهَوَٰتِۖ فَسَوۡفَ يَلۡقَوۡنَ غَيًّا ﴿٥٩﴾

Then came after them the successors who neglected Ṣalāh and followed their lusts and desires. So they will soon face Destruction. (Maryam, 19:59)

This emphasis on Ṣalāh came in Makkah (in the 5th year of Prophethood) about five years before the five daily prayers were ordained. After narrating the stories of many prophets, we are told how deviations came in their followers. The prophets had shown the Straight Path. With the passage of time, their followers were overcome by lusts and turned away from this path. And the first error they committed, which finally led to this tragic result, was being negligent in ṣalāh. A famous hadith gives the same message. Ṣalāh is the pillar of *dīn*, the Islamic way of life. Whoever destroys it destroys his *dīn*. In other words one cannot build an Islamic life, an Islamic community, an Islamic institution, or an Islamic government while neglecting or weakening this pillar.

In one of his circulars Sayyidnā ʿUmar ibn al-Khaṭṭāb رضي الله عنه sent instructions to all his administrators saying, "In my opinion, ṣalāh is the most important of your obligations. Whoever takes good care of it and safeguards it safeguards his religion and whoever neglects it will neglect other things even more." He then added instructions about the times for the five ṣalāhs and admonition against dozing off before Isha.[3]

This letter from the ruler of a vast empire to the officials of his government—shall we call it Executive Order?—gives us a lot to reflect upon. For ṣalāh is among the most emphasized

3 Nāfiʿ in *Muwaṭṭā Imām Mālik*, وقوت الصلاة [Timings of Ṣalāh].

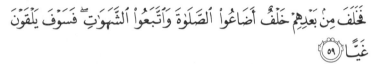

Juz Seventeen

Sūrah al-Ambiyā'

This sūrah narrates the stories of many prophets to highlight the central message of Islam and the urgency with which one must turn to it. This is captured in the following āyahs.

ٱقْتَرَبَ لِلنَّاسِ حِسَابُهُمْ وَهُمْ فِى غَفْلَةٍ مُّعْرِضُونَ ﴿١﴾

Closer draws unto men their reckoning: and yet they remain stubbornly heedless (of its approach). (Al-Ambiyā', 21:1)

The moment of reckoning will come unannounced to each one of us. And for humanity as a whole, too, it keeps coming closer. Yet we are too preoccupied with all the distractions to pay attention.

كُلُّ نَفْسٍ ذَآئِقَةُ ٱلْمَوْتِ ۗ وَنَبْلُوكُم بِٱلشَّرِّ وَٱلْخَيْرِ فِتْنَةً ۖ وَإِلَيْنَا تُرْجَعُونَ ﴿٣٥﴾

Every human being is bound to taste death; and We test you (all) through the bad and the good (things of life) by way of trial: and unto Us you all must return. (Al-Ambiyā', 21:35)

Both the good and the bad things in life are just a test. Those who remember Allāh all the time, are grateful in the case of the first and patient in the case of the second, and never cross the boundaries set by Him in all situations in life, will be winners. Others will be losers.

وَنَضَعُ ٱلْمَوَٰزِينَ ٱلْقِسْطَ لِيَوْمِ ٱلْقِيَـٰمَةِ فَلَا تُظْلَمُ نَفْسٌ شَيْـًٔا ۖ
وَإِن كَانَ مِثْقَالَ حَبَّةٍ مِّنْ خَرْدَلٍ أَتَيْنَا بِهَا ۗ وَكَفَىٰ بِنَا
حَـٰسِبِينَ ﴿٤٧﴾

But We shall set up just balance-scales on Resurrection Day, and no human being shall be wronged in the least: for though there be (in him but) the weight of a mustard-seed (of good or evil), We shall bring it forth; and none can take count as We do! (Al-Ambiyā', 21:47)

Nothing will escape this accounting. We should never belittle a good deed, nor be careless about committing a seemingly minor sin. For all our good and bad deeds, big and small, will be in our books of accounts.

The Mission of the Islamic State

ٱلَّذِينَ إِن مَّكَّنَّـٰهُمْ فِى ٱلْأَرْضِ أَقَامُوا۟ ٱلصَّلَوٰةَ وَءَاتَوُا۟ ٱلزَّكَوٰةَ
وَأَمَرُوا۟ بِٱلْمَعْرُوفِ وَنَهَوْا۟ عَنِ ٱلْمُنكَرِ ۗ وَلِلَّهِ عَـٰقِبَةُ ٱلْأُمُورِ ﴿٤١﴾

(They are) those who, if We give them power in the land, establish Ṣalāh, pay Zakāh, enjoin the right and forbid wrong. And with Allāh lies the fate of all matters. (Al-Ḥajj 22:41)

This is the mission statement for the Islamic government. As Yūsuf Ali writes: "'Enjoining the right and forbidding the wrong' is an essential duty of the Muslim Ummah and one of the main purposes for which it has been raised." In contrast the secular democracy, far from making these the main goal of government, would not even permit their pursuit.

Juz Eighteen

Sūrah al-Mu'minūn

Reflections on Falāḥ (Success)

This sūrah begins with the promise of *falāḥ* for the believers who have certain qualities. It ends with the categorical assertion that non-believers will not get falāḥ. The first eleven āyahs specify the type of person who will definitely achieve falāḥ.

Translated as success, falāḥ signifies a state where a person's every wish comes true and at the same he is protected from everything undesirable. This point is also made explicit in other āyahs. "We have been your friends in the worldly life, and (will remain as such) in the Hereafter. And for you here is whatever your souls desire, and for you here is whatever you call for."[1] "And there will be whatever souls desire and that which eyes enjoy. And you will be living in it forever."[2]

The point to ponder is that if everyone can get all their wishes fulfilled, this could also potentially lead to chaos.

1 *Al-Qur'ān*, Fuṣṣilat 41:31.
2 *Al-Qur'ān*, al-Zukhruf 43:71.

People, after all, are capable of harboring wild wishes! The answer is that only those people will be admitted to Paradise who can handle such a privilege with responsibility, who have purified themselves thoroughly and developed a personality that is qualified to get such a blank check.

Paradise is an exclusive place. Not in the sense that it is reserved for a specific race or nationality or color or economic standing. But in the sense that it is meant only for those who have developed the required personal qualities. It is a beautiful place, more beautiful than the most beautiful place the human mind can even imagine. It is meant for people who have developed an inner beauty. Unlike physical beauty which may be inherited, this is the beauty of the soul which is to be *acquired*—through the purification of one's intentions and actions.

The qualities mentioned in this sūrah (āyah 1-11) should be read with this perspective in mind. This is not a disjointed list of some things that believers are supposed to do; the qualities paint the portrait of the God fearing and God conscious personality that is always seeking good and avoiding evil. We should be judging ourselves not only on the specific qualities listed here but also on how close we are to that ideal personality to see how far we are from true and eternal success.

Qualities for Attaining Falāḥ

The listed qualities are:

A) They are believers.[3] This is the key quality. The success in the Hereafter belongs only to the believers. The point is further emphasized in the end of this sūrah, where it says: "Lo! Disbelievers will not be successful."[4] Paradise is not

3 *Al-Qur'ān*, al-Mu'minūn 23:1.

4 *Al-Qur'ān*, al-Mu'minūn 23:117.

something that will be given away to those who do not even believe in it and are not even seeking it.

B) They concentrate their attention in humbleness when offering ṣalāh (prayers).[5] This is the state of their prayer. Concentration and humbleness mark it, and with the frequency of ṣalāh in their daily life, make these the overriding parts of their personality.

C) They keep themselves away from vain things.[6] They stay away not only from sins, but also from vain pursuits and useless and purposeless activities. They know the value of their time and their resources and do not waste any of them on things that will not contribute to their success.

D) They are performers of Zakāh.[7] This refers to self purification as well as the purification of one's wealth through the charitable donation normally known as Zakāh.

E) They guard their chastity.[8] They stay away from all extramarital sex and things that can lead to it.

F) They honestly look after their trusts and covenants.[9] They are a people for whom talk is not cheap. When they give their word, they honor it. Their pledges are solid. They are honorable people in their dealings with everyone.

G) They (strictly) guard their prayers.[10] The desirable traits are bracketed with references to ṣalāh, thus indicating that it is the pillar of the successful personality. A Muslim negligent in his prayers is far from the model of success that Islam espouses.

5 *Al-Qur'ān*, al-Mu'minūn 23:2.
6 *Al-Qur'ān*, al-Mu'minūn 23:3.
7 *Al-Qur'ān*, al-Mu'minūn 23:4.
8 *Al-Qur'ān*, al-Mu'minūn 23:5.
9 *Al-Qur'ān*, al-Mu'minūn 23:8.
10 *Al-Qur'ān*, al-Mu'minūn 23:9.

Sūrah an-Nūr: Hijab

One of the key qualities for eternal success mentioned in the previous sūrah was guarding chastity. This sūrah further amplifies on it and gives commands both for the preservation of that chastity and for the punishment when it is violated. It begins with the punishment for fornication, followed by punishment for slandering a chaste woman or man. These are two of the four *Ḥudūd* laws, which are not subject to any change with the passage of time. The other two Ḥudūd Laws deal with punishments for theft and consuming alcohol.

It also deals with the slander of Sayyidah 'Ā'ishah رضي الله عنها by the hypocrites, rebuking them and testifying to her chastity.

It continues to give commands for the preservation of ḥayā in the social life of the Muslim community. This forms the essential Islamic "sex education" course. And a key component of that course is contained in the following two āyahs.

قُل لِّلْمُؤْمِنِينَ يَغُضُّوا۟ مِنْ أَبْصَـٰرِهِمْ وَيَحْفَظُوا۟ فُرُوجَهُمْ ۚ ذَٰلِكَ أَزْكَىٰ
لَهُمْ ۗ إِنَّ ٱللَّهَ خَبِيرٌۢ بِمَا يَصْنَعُونَ ﴿٣٠﴾

Tell the believing men that they must restrain their gazes and guard their chastity; it is more decent for them. Surely Allāh is All-Aware of what they do. (An-Nūr, 24:30)

وَقُل لِّلْمُؤْمِنَـٰتِ يَغْضُضْنَ مِنْ أَبْصَـٰرِهِنَّ وَيَحْفَظْنَ فُرُوجَهُنَّ وَلَا
يُبْدِينَ زِينَتَهُنَّ إِلَّا مَا ظَهَرَ مِنْهَا ۖ وَلْيَضْرِبْنَ بِخُمُرِهِنَّ عَلَىٰ جُيُوبِهِنَّ ۖ
وَلَا يُبْدِينَ زِينَتَهُنَّ إِلَّا لِبُعُولَتِهِنَّ أَوْ ءَابَآئِهِنَّ أَوْ ءَابَآءِ
بُعُولَتِهِنَّ أَوْ أَبْنَآئِهِنَّ أَوْ أَبْنَآءِ بُعُولَتِهِنَّ أَوْ إِخْوَٰنِهِنَّ أَوْ
بَنِىٓ إِخْوَٰنِهِنَّ أَوْ بَنِىٓ أَخَوَٰتِهِنَّ أَوْ نِسَآئِهِنَّ أَوْ مَا مَلَكَتْ أَيْمَـٰنُهُنَّ

أَوِ ٱلتَّٰبِعِينَ غَيْرِ أُوْلِي ٱلْإِرْبَةِ مِنَ ٱلرِّجَالِ أَوِ ٱلطِّفْلِ ٱلَّذِينَ
لَمْ يَظْهَرُوا۟ عَلَىٰ عَوْرَٰتِ ٱلنِّسَآءِ ۖ وَلَا يَضْرِبْنَ بِأَرْجُلِهِنَّ لِيُعْلَمَ مَا
يُخْفِينَ مِن زِينَتِهِنَّ ۚ وَتُوبُوٓا۟ إِلَى ٱللَّهِ جَمِيعًا أَيُّهَ ٱلْمُؤْمِنُونَ لَعَلَّكُمْ
تُفْلِحُونَ ﴿٣١﴾

And tell the believing women that they must restrain their gazes and guard their chastity, and must not expose their adornment, except that which (necessarily) appears thereof, and must wrap their bosoms with their shawls, and must not expose their adornment, except to their husbands or their fathers or the fathers of their husbands, or to their sons or the sons of their husbands, or to their brothers or the sons of their brothers or the sons of their sisters, or to their women, or to those owned by their right hands, or male attendants having no (sexual) urge, or to the children who are not yet conscious of the private parts of women. And let them not stamp their feet in a way that the adornment they conceal is known. And repent to Allāh O believers, all of you, so that you may achieve success. (An-Nūr, 24:31)

The first step toward preserving chastity is the creation of the environment in which temptations are minimized. A woman's beauty is not public property to be enjoyed by one and all. It is a private treasure that has to be kept private. Both men and women have to restrain their gazes so the looks that can potentially start lusts are nipped in the bud. But women have to do more by covering themselves as detailed above.

Ḥayā'

Islam's laws about hijab, its ban against free mixing of men and women, its teachings about gender-relations—all of these reflect a deep concern for *ḥayā*. The only people who will try to water down these injunctions are those who are not fully cognizant of ḥayā's central place in Islamic life and the destruction caused in the society by its absence.

What is ḥayā? It is normally translated as modesty or inhibition but neither word conveys the same idea as ḥayā. Modesty suggests shunning indecent behavior but it also implies bashfulness based on timidity. That is why the adjective based on its opposite, immodest, is sometimes also used as a compliment suggesting courage. Inhibition is defined as: "Conscious or unconscious mechanism whereby unacceptable impulses are suppressed." This is a very neutral definition with no reference to right or wrong. Thus one finds psychiatrists "helping" their patients overcome inhibitions.

In contrast to the moral ambiguity of these words, ḥayā refers to an extremely desirable quality that protects us from all evil. It is a natural feeling that brings us pain at the very idea of committing a wrong.

Along with its unique connotation comes the unique value of ḥayā in Islam. Prophet Muḥammad ﷺ said: "Every religion has a distinct call. For Islam it is ḥayā."[11] Another famous hadith says: "There are more than seventy branches of Īmān (faith). The foremost is the declaration that there is no god except Allāh and the least of it is removing harmful things from the path. And ḥayā is a branch of Īmān."[12] As some Muḥadithīn point out, the number seventy is a figure of speech. What the hadith tells us is that the declaration of faith is the most important part of Īmān but that is not all. Īmān also has to reflect itself in all kinds of actions in real life. Moreover, ḥayā is a centerpiece of most of the actions that Īmān calls for. It is the basic building block of Islamic morality. When it is lost everything is lost.

---

11 Anas رضي الله عنه in *Sunan Ibn Mājah*, كتاب الزهد [Chapter: Zuhd].

12 Abū Hurayrah رضي الله عنه in *Ṣaḥīḥ Muslim*, كتاب الايمان [Chapter: Faith].

Restraining Gazes

The command to restrain gazes is seen today in wholesale violation. In fact women feel they are a greater target of stares on the streets, say, in Karachi or Istanbul than they are in Los Angeles or London. This sad reality then leads some to question the very restrictions being violated. Maybe we can have better morality if all the restrictions are removed?

We need to put this delusion to rest. What we are seeing in Los Angeles or London are better manners and not better morals. The alarming rates of sexual improprieties at every level of the society, from the President on down, at the same time that sexual impropriety is being constantly redefined and narrowed down, are sufficient to put an end to this fanciful thesis.

However it does show that when believers violate Allāh's commands, they may become worse than anybody else in their manners as well. This should not detract us from the fact that the goal of the believers is to excel in both manners *and* morals. This can only be achieved by turning back to Allāh. Once again, we need to start listening to the Qur'ān to get out of this terrible mess.

Juz Nineteen

Friendships

وَيَوْمَ يَعَضُّ ٱلظَّالِمُ عَلَىٰ يَدَيْهِ يَقُولُ يَٰلَيْتَنِى ٱتَّخَذْتُ مَعَ ٱلرَّسُولِ سَبِيلًا
﴿٢٧﴾ يَٰوَيْلَتَىٰ لَيْتَنِى لَمْ أَتَّخِذْ فُلَانًا خَلِيلًا ﴿٢٨﴾ لَّقَدْ أَضَلَّنِى عَنِ ٱلذِّكْرِ
بَعْدَ إِذْ جَآءَنِى ۗ وَكَانَ ٱلشَّيْطَٰنُ لِلْإِنسَٰنِ خَذُولًا ﴿٢٩﴾

And (be mindful of) the Day the wrongdoer will bite his hands saying, "Would that I had taken a path along with the Messenger! Oh, woe to me! Would that I had not taken so-and-so for a friend! He did lead me astray from the Message (of Allāh) after it had come to me! Ah! Satan is but a traitor to man! (Al-Furqān 25:27-29).

This is direct reference to the case of ʿUqbah ibn Abu Muʿayṭ, who accepted Islam then turned back and even spat on the face of the Prophet ﷺ under the pressure of his friend Ubayy ibn Khalaf. Both of them reached an evil end.

But the wording is general and is a reminder that we should never accept as friends those people who may lead us away from the path of the Messenger ﷺ. If we do we'll get nothing but regrets in the end. We should choose friends who will be a positive influence on us, whose friendship will make it easy for us to follow the path of piety and righteousness. A hadith makes it very clear: "Everyone is influenced by his friends, so watch out whom you are befriending."[1]

The Qur'ān and Us

وَقَالَ ٱلرَّسُولُ يَٰرَبِّ إِنَّ قَوْمِى ٱتَّخَذُوا۟ هَٰذَا ٱلْقُرْءَانَ مَهْجُورًا ﴿٣٠﴾

And (on that Day) the Messenger will say: "O my Sustainer! Behold, (some of) my people have come to regard this Qur'ān as a thing to be shunned" (al-Furqān, 25:30)

The reference in my people (qawmī) is to the mushrikīn of Quraysh. But the general wording should give pause to the Muslims whose behavior fits the description. Today we have severed the link between the Qur'ān and our daily life. We do not read it, try to understand it, reflect on it, and make it the guiding light for the individual and collective affairs of our life as we ought to do. To the extent that we are deficient in these obligations, we are liable to be accused as mentioned here. May Allāh protect us from the Qur'ān and the Prophet ﷺ becoming our accusers.

Portrait of Believers

This sūrah ends with another snapshot of the character of believers. As mentioned in the reflections on Sūrah al-Mu'minūn, these should not be seen as so many disjointed commands, but as pointers to the desirable personality. These are the people who can affectionately be called the servants of the Most Merciful.

---

1 Abū Hurayrah رضي الله عنه in *Sunan Abū Dāwūd*, كتاب الأدب [Chapter: Manners].

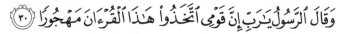

It is also to be noted that the qualities are listed not as goals but accomplishments. These āyahs are not saying, "O believers do this." Rather they are saying, "Believers are already doing this." At other places in the Qur'ān believers have been praised for virtuous acts though they were not commanded to do them anywhere in the Qur'ān. Reflecting on this will enlighten us about both the role of the Prophet ﷺ and that of the Companions. The Companions either learned these qualities directly from the Prophet ﷺ or as a result of Prophetic training, they developed that mindset that automatically led them to the praiseworthy course of action.

Qualities

They walk humbly.[2]
They avoid arguments with the ignorant people.[3]
They spend the nights in worship of Allāh.[4]
They follow the path of moderation in economic matters. They are neither spendthrift nor stingy.[5]
They respect sanctity of life.[6]
They do not commit fornication or adultery.[7]
They do not bear false witness.[8]
They do not turn deaf and dumb to the words of Allāh.[9]
They seek and pray for raising a family based on piety and virtue.[10]

---

2 *Al-Qur'ān*, al-Furqān 25:63.

3 *Al-Qur'ān*, al-Furqān 25:63.

4 *Al-Qur'ān*, al-Furqān 25:64.

5 *Al-Qur'ān*, al-Furqān 25:67.

6 *Al-Qur'ān*, al-Furqān 25:68.

7 *Al-Qur'ān*, al-Furqān 25:68.

8 *Al-Qur'ān*, al-Furqān 25:72.

9 *Al-Qur'ān*, al-Furqān 25:73.

10 *Al-Qur'ān*, al-Furqān 25:74.

Pharaoh and "Political Islam"

﴿٣٣﴾ قَالَ لِلْمَلَإِ حَوْلَهُۥٓ إِنَّ هَٰذَا لَسَٰحِرٌ عَلِيمٌ ﴿٣٤﴾ يُرِيدُ أَن يُخْرِجَكُم مِّنْ
أَرْضِكُم بِسِحْرِهِۦ فَمَاذَا تَأْمُرُونَ ﴿٣٥﴾

He (Pharaoh) said to the chiefs around him "This man is certainly an expert sorcerer". He wants to expel you from your land with his sorcery. So what do you suggest?" (Ash-Shuʿarā' 26:34-35)

The encounters of Prophet Mūsa عليه السلام with the Pharaoh are reported in several places in the Qur'ān including here. It is obvious that both Pharaoh and his expert advisers were looking at the "problem" of Prophet Mūsa عليه السلام as a political problem. For them it was all about a power struggle. They painted Prophet Mūsa عليه السلام as the leader of a "political Islam" that threatened to drive them from power and fashioned their strategy and propaganda campaigns accordingly. In sūrah Taha we see them calling Prophet Mūsa عليه السلام as a threat to their superior lifestyle. "Said they, 'Certainly, these two are sorcerers who wish to drive you out from your land, and do away with your excellent way of life.'"[11]

This preoccupation with political analysis became the big barrier that kept the Pharaoh and his advisers from seeing the Truth.

11 *Al-Qur'ān*, Ṭāhā 20:63.

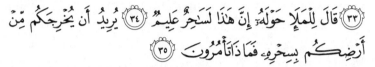

Juz Twenty

Sūrah al-Qaṣaṣ

This is the last sūrah revealed before hijrah; its āyah 85 was revealed when the Prophet ﷺ had already started his journey to Madinah. This was a heart breaking departure and he was consoled that Allāh would be bringing him back to this city as a conqueror. This happened within a decade although at that time there were no apparent clues leading to this result.

In preparation for the encounter with Jews in Madinah, the first 43 āyahs give a detailed account of the life of Prophet Mūsā ﵇ not given anywhere else in the Qur'ān. The parallels between the lives of Prophet Muḥammad ﷺ and that of Prophet Mūsā ﵇ are unmistakable. Prophet Mūsā ﵇ had also left his home when his life was threatened. He was later brought back and ultimately the Pharaoh was drowned. The account thus provides assurance for the Prophet ﷺ and admonishment for the unbelievers.

Qārūn (Korah) and Others of His Ilk

إِنَّ قَٰرُونَ كَانَ مِن قَوْمِ مُوسَىٰ فَبَغَىٰ عَلَيْهِمْ ۖ وَءَاتَيْنَٰهُ مِنَ ٱلْكُنُوزِ مَآ إِنَّ
مَفَاتِحَهُۥ لَتَنُوٓأُ بِٱلْعُصْبَةِ أُو۟لِى ٱلْقُوَّةِ إِذْ قَالَ لَهُۥ قَوْمُهُۥ لَا تَفْرَحْ ۖ إِنَّ ٱللَّهَ
لَا يُحِبُّ ٱلْفَرِحِينَ ﴿٧٦﴾ وَٱبْتَغِ فِيمَآ ءَاتَىٰكَ ٱللَّهُ ٱلدَّارَ ٱلْءَاخِرَةَ ۖ وَلَا
تَنسَ نَصِيبَكَ مِنَ ٱلدُّنْيَا ۖ وَأَحْسِن كَمَآ أَحْسَنَ ٱللَّهُ إِلَيْكَ ۖ وَلَا
تَبْغِ ٱلْفَسَادَ فِى ٱلْأَرْضِ ۖ إِنَّ ٱللَّهَ لَا يُحِبُّ ٱلْمُفْسِدِينَ ﴿٧٧﴾ قَالَ إِنَّمَآ أُوتِيتُهُۥ
عَلَىٰ عِلْمٍ عِندِىٓ ۚ أَوَلَمْ يَعْلَمْ أَنَّ ٱللَّهَ قَدْ أَهْلَكَ مِن قَبْلِهِۦ مِنَ ٱلْقُرُونِ مَنْ
هُوَ أَشَدُّ مِنْهُ قُوَّةً وَأَكْثَرُ جَمْعًا ۚ وَلَا يُسْـَٔلُ عَن ذُنُوبِهِمُ ٱلْمُجْرِمُونَ
﴿٧٨﴾ فَخَرَجَ عَلَىٰ قَوْمِهِۦ فِى زِينَتِهِۦ ۖ قَالَ ٱلَّذِينَ يُرِيدُونَ ٱلْحَيَوٰةَ ٱلدُّنْيَا
يَٰلَيْتَ لَنَا مِثْلَ مَآ أُوتِىَ قَٰرُونُ إِنَّهُۥ لَذُو حَظٍّ عَظِيمٍ ﴿٧٩﴾ وَقَالَ
ٱلَّذِينَ أُوتُوا۟ ٱلْعِلْمَ وَيْلَكُمْ ثَوَابُ ٱللَّهِ خَيْرٌ لِّمَنْ ءَامَنَ وَعَمِلَ
صَٰلِحًا وَلَا يُلَقَّىٰهَآ إِلَّا ٱلصَّٰبِرُونَ ﴿٨٠﴾ فَخَسَفْنَا بِهِۦ وَبِدَارِهِ ٱلْأَرْضَ
فَمَا كَانَ لَهُۥ مِن فِئَةٍ يَنصُرُونَهُۥ مِن دُونِ ٱللَّهِ وَمَا كَانَ مِنَ ٱلْمُنتَصِرِينَ
﴿٨١﴾ وَأَصْبَحَ ٱلَّذِينَ تَمَنَّوْا۟ مَكَانَهُۥ بِٱلْأَمْسِ يَقُولُونَ وَيْكَأَنَّ ٱللَّهَ
يَبْسُطُ ٱلرِّزْقَ لِمَن يَشَآءُ مِنْ عِبَادِهِۦ وَيَقْدِرُ ۖ لَوْلَآ أَن مَّنَّ ٱللَّهُ عَلَيْنَا
لَخَسَفَ بِنَا ۖ وَيْكَأَنَّهُۥ لَا يُفْلِحُ ٱلْكَٰفِرُونَ ﴿٨٢﴾

Indeed Qārūn (Korah) was from the people of Mūsā, then he rebelled against them. And We had given him treasures such that the very keys of them were too heavy a burden for a company of men endowed with strength. (Remember) when his people said to him, "Do not exult. Surely, Allāh loves not those that exult. And seek the (betterment of) the Ultimate Abode with what Allāh has given to you, and do not neglect your share from this world, and do good as Allāh did good to you, and do not seek to make mischief in the land.

Surely, Allāh does not like the mischief-makers." Answered he: "This (wealth) has been given to me only by virtue of the knowledge that is in me!" Did he not know that God had destroyed (the arrogant of) many a generation that preceded him—people who were greater than he in power, and richer in what they had amassed? But such as are lost in sin may not be asked about their sins (for ascertaining their sins). And so he went forth before his people in all his pomp; (and) those who cared only for the life of this world would say, "Oh, if we but had the like of what Qārūn has been given! He is a man of great fortune indeed!" But those who had been granted true knowledge said: "Woe unto you! Merit in the sight of Allāh is by far the best for any who attains to faith and does what is right: but none save the patient in adversity can ever achieve this (blessing)." And thereupon We caused the earth to swallow him and his dwelling; and he had none to help him against Allāh, nor was he of those who could defend themselves. And on the morrow, those who but yesterday had longed to be in his place exclaimed: "Alas (for our not having been aware) that it is indeed Allāh (alone) who grants abundant sustenance, or gives it in scant measure, unto whichever He wills of His creatures! Had not Allāh been gracious to us, He might have caused (the earth) to swallow us, too! Alas (for our having forgotten) that those who deny the truth can never attain to a happy state!" (Al-Qaṣaṣ 28:76-82)

The account of Qārūn (Korah in the Bible) is given at the end of the sūrah. Qārūn is the personification of the possible evils of wealth. He was given tremendous wealth, which got to his head. He believed, as many do today, that his economic success was the result of his own knowledge and smarts. Little did he realize that for every smart person who has struck it rich, there are many smarter people who have not. How many are the economically successful who can see that their success was the result of simply being at the right place at the right time?

Failure to comprehend that our wealth or lack thereof is a test decreed by Allāh according to His plan leads to the other common evil. The surplus wealth begs to be put on display to advertize the superiority of those who hold it. Qārūn did the same. And it did take its toll on the shallow people who are captivated by this world and have not received the revealed knowledge. (Such are the people being produced by our education systems today). They said Qārūn had got it made and wished they had the same. The people of knowledge (i.e revealed knowledge) tried to talk sense to them telling them the real important things were faith and virtue. The truth of this was finally realized by the first group when Qārūn was buried alive along with his wealth.

Wealth also took another toll on the poor Qārūn. He belonged to a colonized people (Bani Israel) and had accepted to work for the Pharaoh as his agent to control his own people. He betrayed his people and became an oppressor for them—because his narrowly conceived vested interests dictated so.

We can see the dark character of Qārūn, the agent, in the history of colonized people to this day. We can also see the character of Qārūn, the filthy rich, in every society.

Successful Personality

تِلْكَ ٱلدَّارُ ٱلْءَاخِرَةُ نَجْعَلُهَا لِلَّذِينَ لَا يُرِيدُونَ عُلُوًّا فِى ٱلْأَرْضِ وَلَا فَسَادًا ۚ
وَٱلْعَٰقِبَةُ لِلْمُتَّقِينَ ﴿٨٣﴾

As for that Ultimate Abode (the Hereafter), We assign it to those who do not intend haughtiness on earth nor mischief. And the (best) end is for the God-fearing. (Al-Qaṣaṣ, 28:83)

The eternal success belongs to the good people. Their defining characteristic is that they seek neither oppression of others nor corruption. They are a God-fearing people or *muttaqī* in the special Qur'ānic terminology.

Nurturing of taqwā is a central Islamic goal. The Qur'ānic guidance is beneficial only for those who have taqwā.[1] The purpose of fasting is also to develop taqwā.[2] All acts of virtue are performed by the muttaqīn (plural of muttaqī).[3] Paradise has been created for the muttaqīn.[4]

Limits of Parental Rights

وَوَصَّيْنَا ٱلْإِنسَٰنَ بِوَٰلِدَيْهِ حُسْنًا ۖ وَإِن جَٰهَدَاكَ لِتُشْرِكَ بِى مَا لَيْسَ لَكَ بِهِۦ
عِلْمٌ فَلَا تُطِعْهُمَآ ۚ إِلَىَّ مَرْجِعُكُمْ فَأُنَبِّئُكُم بِمَا كُنتُمْ تَعْمَلُونَ ﴿٨﴾

We have charged man to do good to his parents. But if they insist upon you that you associate with Me that of which you have no knowledge, then do not obey them. To Me is your return; then I shall tell you what you were doing. (Al-'Ankabūt 29:8)

The persons who have the greatest right on us are our parents. Yet when this right impinges on the right of Allāh to be worshipped alone, it will be disregarded. It follows that rights of other people will be disregarded even more when they conflict with the commands of Allāh. There is absolutely no obedience to other people that results in disobedience to Allāh.

---

1 *Al-Qur'ān*, al-Baqarah 2:2.

2 *Al-Qur'ān*, al-Baqarah 2:183.

3 *Al-Qur'ān*, al-Baqarah 2:177.

4 *Al-Qur'ān*, Āli 'Imran 3:133.

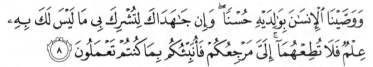

A Great Reassurance

وَٱلَّذِينَ جَٰهَدُوا۟ فِينَا لَنَهْدِيَنَّهُمْ سُبُلَنَا ۚ وَإِنَّ ٱللَّهَ لَمَعَ ٱلْمُحْسِنِينَ ﴿٦٩﴾

But as for those who strive hard in Our cause—We shall most certainly guide them onto paths that lead unto Us: for, behold, Allāh is indeed with the doers of good. (Al-'Ankabūt, 29:69)

This āyah holds great reassurance for all those who may find hurdles in obeying Allāh. When doors seem to be locked and all options look bad, let us have faith. We should turn to Allāh seeking His help and do the best we can under the circumstances. And we will find a way out with help from totally unexpected sources. The Qur'ānic words are very emphatic. Let us find comfort in their great promise. If we keep this āyah in front of us, we'll never lose hope, no matter what the current circumstances.

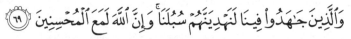

Juz Twenty One

Sūrah ar-Rūm

This sūrah begins with two predictions. One was for the victory of Romans over the Persians after they had been nearly vanquished by the latter. Simultaneously, it was predicted, Muslims would gain victory over the Quraysh. Both would take place in less than a decade. Both looked impossible at the time. Both came to pass as predicted. In this alone there is ample proof for open minded people that the Qur'ān is the Word of Allāh.

Limits of Scientific Knowledge

يَعۡلَمُونَ ظَٰهِرٗا مِّنَ ٱلۡحَيَوٰةِ ٱلدُّنۡيَا وَهُمۡ عَنِ ٱلۡأٓخِرَةِ هُمۡ غَٰفِلُونَ ٧

They know but the outer surface of this world's life, whereas of the ultimate things they are utterly unaware. (Ar-Rūm, 30:7)

This is a general comment on the limits of human knowledge acquired through sense perception and logical reasoning—in other words, scientific knowledge. This knowledge is based only on the observable phenomenon, whether observed with the help of instruments or without. But there is much more to life than the observable spectrum. The victory of Romans over the Persians within a decade, was beyond all human calculations.

Realizing the limits of human knowledge is a prerequisite for opening our hearts and minds to revealed knowledge. As we are reminded elsewhere in the Qur'ān: "of knowledge it is only a little that has been given to you."[1] Without this realization, the scientific knowledge—though useful and important in its limited scope—acquires a place in our life for which it is not qualified. It then leads to the disaster called scientism, when it becomes the final judge and arbiter of everything in life. This āyah is a powerful tool to break that hegemony of science.

Music and Distractions

وَمِنَ ٱلنَّاسِ مَن يَشْتَرِى لَهْوَ ٱلْحَدِيثِ لِيُضِلَّ عَن سَبِيلِ ٱللَّهِ بِغَيْرِ عِلْمٍ
وَيَتَّخِذَهَا هُزُوًا ۚ أُو۟لَـٰٓئِكَ لَهُمْ عَذَابٌ مُّهِينٌ ﴿٦﴾

But there are, among men, those who purchase distracting amusements, without knowledge (or meaning), to mislead (men) from the Path of Allāh and throw ridicule (on the Path): For such people there is a disgraceful punishment. (Luqmān, 31:6)

This includes all distractions—music, video games, movies, television entertainment programs—that fit the description in terms of their effect. There is a place for recreation in life, when its purpose is to rejuvenate us and prepare us to better face the serious tasks in life. But when recreation becomes a goal in itself and a means of diverting us from the Path of

1 *Al-Qur'ān*, al-Isrā' 17:85.

Allāh then it is a curse. This is one of the āyahs that show the prohibition of music and all other distractions in Islam.[2]

Today the human weakness to fall for such diversions has been exploited in an unprecedented manner with the help of machines. When music could only be produced by a live person working in real time, no one, no matter how rich, could surround himself with music at all hours of the day and night. Today no one is safe from it at any hour of the day or night. No place or time is immune.

Probably that explains why we see such an increase in the occurrence of disasters, both natural and man-made, today. The disasters are reminders so we leave our state of forgetfulness and turn to Allāh. The disasters have increased because the distractions have increased. May Allāh protect us from both.

2 For a fuller discussion of this āyah, see Baig, Khalid. *Slippery Stone: An Inquiry into Islam's Stance on Music.* (California: Open Mind Press). 107-115.

Juz Twenty Two

Sūrah al-Aḥzāb: Reflections on Hijab

In this sūrah, which was revealed at the time of the battle of the trench (also known as the battle of Aḥzāb), hijab was introduced as a formal requirement for Muslim women. This was a revolutionary change. The Arab society of the time was a stranger to the idea of segregation and hijab as mentioned in āyah 33 below. This era was declared as a dark era of ignorance (*al-Jāhiliyyah al-Ūlā*, or the earlier Jāhiliyyah) and the new Muslim community was asked to move away from its cultural and social practices. The qualifier Ūlā (earlier) implies the prophesy of a later Jāhiliyyah, and what we are witnessing today in the modern world fits the bill.

Those who are trying to reconcile Islam to this modern Jāhiliyyah have been working hard to water down these teachings. Among their arguments is that these āyahs were meant only for the wives of the Prophet ﷺ. Little do they realize that the household of the Prophet ﷺ was charged with becoming the model that the rest of the community would follow, for a revolutionary change in such practices required the presence of cultural leaders. A careful reading of the following āyahs will make that amply clear.

يَٰنِسَآءَ ٱلنَّبِيِّ لَسۡتُنَّ كَأَحَدٖ مِّنَ ٱلنِّسَآءِ إِنِ ٱتَّقَيۡتُنَّۚ فَلَا تَخۡضَعۡنَ بِٱلۡقَوۡلِ
فَيَطۡمَعَ ٱلَّذِي فِي قَلۡبِهِۦ مَرَضٞ وَقُلۡنَ قَوۡلٗا مَّعۡرُوفٗا ٣٢

O wives of the prophet, you are not like any other women, if you observe taqwā (righteousness). So, do not be too soft in your speech, lest someone having disease in his heart develop fancies (about you); and do speak with appropriate words. (Al-Aḥzāb 33:32)

This āyah makes two points. First, the wives of the Prophet ﷺ are at a level above other women because of *taqwā*. Second, in talking to other men their talk should avoid display of female charms to prevent the development of any fancies. Are we to believe that developing *taqwā* and preempting the possibility of developing lust were only the concern of the wives of the Prophet ﷺ?

وَقَرۡنَ فِي بُيُوتِكُنَّ وَلَا تَبَرَّجۡنَ تَبَرُّجَ ٱلۡجَٰهِلِيَّةِ ٱلۡأُولَىٰۖ وَأَقِمۡنَ
ٱلصَّلَوٰةَ وَءَاتِينَ ٱلزَّكَوٰةَ وَأَطِعۡنَ ٱللَّهَ وَرَسُولَهُۥٓۚ إِنَّمَا يُرِيدُ ٱللَّهُ
لِيُذۡهِبَ عَنكُمُ ٱلرِّجۡسَ أَهۡلَ ٱلۡبَيۡتِ وَيُطَهِّرَكُمۡ تَطۡهِيرٗا ٣٣

Remain in your homes, and do not flaunt your charms as they used to flaunt them in the days of earlier ignorance; and establish Ṣalāh, and pay Zakāh, and obey Allāh and His Messenger. Allāh only intends to keep (all sorts of) filth away from you, O members of the family (of the prophet), and to make you pure through a perfect purification. (Al-Aḥzāb, 33:33)

Here again the question will be whether breaking from the Jāhiliyyah practices was only required of the wives of the

Prophet ﷺ. What about Ṣalāh and Zakāh? Why are they mentioned in this "exclusive" directive?

وَإِذَا سَأَلْتُمُوهُنَّ مَتَٰعًا فَسْـَٔلُوهُنَّ مِن وَرَآءِ حِجَابٍ ۚ ذَٰلِكُمْ أَطْهَرُ لِقُلُوبِكُمْ وَقُلُوبِهِنَّ

And when you ask anything from them (the blessed wives of the Prophet), ask them from behind a curtain. That is better for the purity of your hearts and their hearts. (Al-Aḥzāb, 33:53)

We can continue the same question here. Was the purity of hearts only needed for the wives?

يَٰٓأَيُّهَا ٱلنَّبِىُّ قُل لِّأَزْوَٰجِكَ وَبَنَاتِكَ وَنِسَآءِ ٱلْمُؤْمِنِينَ يُدْنِينَ عَلَيْهِنَّ مِن جَلَٰبِيبِهِنَّ ۚ ذَٰلِكَ أَدْنَىٰٓ أَن يُعْرَفْنَ فَلَا يُؤْذَيْنَ ۗ وَكَانَ ٱللَّهُ غَفُورًا رَّحِيمًا ﴿٥٩﴾

O Prophet, tell your wives and your daughters and the women of the believers that they should draw down their shawls over them. That will make it more likely that they are recognized, hence not teased. And Allāh is Most-Forgiving, Very-Merciful. (Al-Aḥzāb, 33:59)

This āyah now extends the command to all Muslim women although wives and daughters of the Prophet ﷺ are again mentioned first. The reason for earlier specific addresses to them should now be obvious to everyone. They were charged to lead the cultural revolution—as they in fact did. Hijab became a symbol of all Muslim women, not just that of the wives of the Prophet ﷺ. The ban on free mixing extended to the entire community. Islam established separate spheres for men and women, and Muslim societies throughout the centuries held fast to this norm.

Satan: The Eternal Enemy of Human Beings

إِنَّ ٱلشَّيْطَٰنَ لَكُمْ عَدُوٌّ فَٱتَّخِذُوهُ عَدُوًّا ۚ إِنَّمَا يَدْعُوا۟ حِزْبَهُۥ لِيَكُونُوا۟ مِنْ أَصْحَٰبِ ٱلسَّعِيرِ ﴿٦﴾

Surely Shayṭān (Satan) is an enemy to you: so treat him as an enemy. He only invites his adherents, that they may become Companions of the Blazing Fire. (Fāṭir 35:6)

There is only one permanent external enemy of human beings—Shayṭān (Satan), also referred to as Iblīs or the Devil. He is a sworn and irreconcilable enemy. Other external enemies, among humans, become enemies to the extent that they become agents for this eternal enemy. So there is a huge difference between the two classes of enemies. We do fight the human enemies when that becomes absolutely necessary, but we can also try to win them over with good character. Thus in sūrah Fuṣṣilat we are told how to turn enemies into friends: "Good and evil are not equal. Repel (evil) with what is best, and you will see that the one between whom and you there was enmity (will become) as though he was a close friend." [1]

And if they stop following Satan, then former enemies become brothers as has been seen throughout the history of Islam.

Not so with Satan. The Qur'ān reminds us repeatedly that Satan is a manifest enemy. Here, again, it is commanding us to make sure we treat him as enemy. We must fight him and protect ourselves from his cunning ways all our life. No appeasement, no compromises, no truce, no let up in the fight. Never.

While Satan invites us to unbelief, he also tempts us to commit all sorts of sins. However some sins have been

1 *Al-Qur'ān*, Fuṣṣilat 41:34.

specifically mentioned as high on the agenda of Satan. These include nudity and obscenities, consumption of alcohol and ḥarām food items, gambling, and extravagance. A hadith mentions breaking up the family and sowing dissension between husband and wife as being on top of the satanic agenda. To the extent that these are prevalent in a society, that society is under satanic influence. And the Believers have their job cut out for them to fight the enemy plans.

The True People of Knowledge

أَلَمْ تَرَ أَنَّ ٱللَّهَ أَنزَلَ مِنَ ٱلسَّمَآءِ مَآءً فَأَخْرَجْنَا بِهِۦ ثَمَرَٰتٍ مُّخْتَلِفًا أَلْوَٰنُهَا ۚ
وَمِنَ ٱلْجِبَالِ جُدَدٌۢ بِيضٌ وَحُمْرٌ مُّخْتَلِفٌ أَلْوَٰنُهَا وَغَرَابِيبُ سُودٌ
﴿٢٧﴾ وَمِنَ ٱلنَّاسِ وَٱلدَّوَآبِّ وَٱلْأَنْعَٰمِ مُخْتَلِفٌ أَلْوَٰنُهُۥ كَذَٰلِكَ ۗ
إِنَّمَا يَخْشَى ٱللَّهَ مِنْ عِبَادِهِ ٱلْعُلَمَٰٓؤُا۟ ۗ إِنَّ ٱللَّهَ عَزِيزٌ غَفُورٌ ﴿٢٨﴾

Did you not see that Allāh sends down water from the sky whereby We bring forth fruits having different colors. And among the mountains there are tracks, white and red- of different colors, and (others) utterly black. And among humans and beasts and cattle, there are those having different colors as well. Even so only those of His servants fear Allāh who have knowledge; surely Allāh is All-mighty, All-forgiving. (Fāṭir, 35:27-28)

After mentioning the great diversity in plant and animal kingdoms, in geological formations and in humans, this āyah goes on to give a new perspective on the knowledgeable and hence on knowledge itself. The examples mentioned are all the subjects of science. But not all those who would study and master them will have true knowledge, for true knowledge produces consciousness and fear of Allāh. If the latter is absent, so is the former. Such a person will remain an ignorant person in the sight of Allāh, no matter how many professional degrees and awards he or she has accumulated.

Juz Twenty Three

Ignoring the Signs of Allāh

وَمَا تَأْتِيهِم مِّنْ ءَايَةٍ مِّنْ ءَايَٰتِ رَبِّهِمْ إِلَّا كَانُوا۟ عَنْهَا مُعْرِضِينَ ﴿٤٦﴾

There comes to them no sign from the signs of your Lord, but they turn away from it. (Yāsīn, 36:46)

The Prophet ﷺ called sūrah Yāsīn the heart of the Qur'ān because it encapsulates the essential message of the Qur'ān and the signs in the universe that point to its truth in a very powerful way.

Yet the signs cannot benefit those who are bent on ignoring them. After mentioning various signs of Allāh (dead earth that comes to life with rain[1], night and day and sun and moon[2], ships and other means of travel[3]), it points out the state of self-imposed ignorance whereby human beings refuse to learn from the signs. This nonchalance results in foolish

---

1 *Al-Qur'ān*, Yāsīn 36:33.

2 *Al-Qur'ān*, Yāsīn 36:38-40.

3 *Al-Qur'ān*, Yāsīn 36:42.

argumentation from them, mentioned in the next two āyahs. (Why should we feed the poor, God could have fed them if He wanted? And when is this resurrection after death going to take place?) The answer is to shake them out of this frivolity by giving a glimpse of the Hereafter where the sinners will be separated from the pious. The difference between the former's doom and the latter's bliss is not something that any sensible person can brush aside lightly.

The charge of ignoring the signs applies to those who pay no attention to them as well as those who study them in great depth but with a closed mindset that has already decided that this is a creation without a Creator and a design without a Designer. Their study does not lead them to God, because of its prior assumptions and predetermined conclusions. This applies to almost all study of science even in the Muslim classrooms today because they just ape the methods and philosophies of ignorant science leaders. This is a similar message to what was given in sūrah Yūsuf[4] and should be a point of much concern for Muslim educators and scientists today.

Did Man Create gods?

قَالَ أَتَعْبُدُونَ مَا تَنْحِتُونَ ﴿٩٥﴾

He answered: "Do you worship something that you (yourselves) have carved, (Al-Ṣāffāt, 37:95)

Atheists, new and old, have declared that man created God. With this they laughingly assure themselves that they have satisfactorily answered the question as to who created man. But this absurdity has a basis, which the Qur'ān points out

4 *Al-Qur'ān*, Yūsuf 12:105

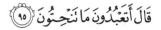

here. Man, in fact, has created gods. Whether it is the physical statues of deities or the false ideas about gods, they are all human creations. They result when we surrender to our own lusts, desires, and wishes. That however does not negate the existence of the one True God who created us.

Atheism took root in the non-Muslim world, where its leaders only saw the false gods of human creation and decided that that was the entire story. In contrast those who read the Qur'ān with an open mind will come in conversation with the one True God.

Worship has always been a common practice in all human societies. But we have two options about it. We can worship the one True God who created us or we can worship the false gods of our own creation—including the "no God" of atheism.

Doubt the Hereafter? Answer This.

أَمْ نَجْعَلُ ٱلَّذِينَ ءَامَنُوا۟ وَعَمِلُوا۟ ٱلصَّٰلِحَٰتِ كَٱلْمُفْسِدِينَ فِى ٱلْأَرْضِ أَمْ نَجْعَلُ ٱلْمُتَّقِينَ كَٱلْفُجَّارِ ﴿٢٨﴾

Shall We treat those who believe and do righteous deeds the same as those who commit mischief on the earth? Shall We make the God-fearing equal to the sinners? (Ṣād 38:28)

This is the question that everyone who rejects or harbors doubts about the Hereafter must answer. Allāh is just and justice demands the existence of the Hereafter where everyone will be rewarded or punished for their good and bad deeds. Those who reject or doubt the Hereafter necessarily believe in an unjust world.

Juz Twenty Four

Sincerity

Sincerity and exclusive devotion to Allāh alone is the central tenet of Islam. In sūrah al-Zumar, which was revealed before the migration to Abyssinia and which is a concise statement of what Islam is all about, this tenet is repeated four times. It begins with a command and a statement of principle:

إِنَّآ أَنزَلْنَآ إِلَيْكَ ٱلْكِتَٰبَ بِٱلْحَقِّ فَٱعْبُدِ ٱللَّهَ مُخْلِصًا لَّهُ ٱلدِّينَ ﴿٢﴾
أَلَا لِلَّهِ ٱلدِّينُ ٱلْخَالِصُ

Surely We have revealed the Book to you with truth; so worship Allāh making your submission exclusive for Him. Remember, Allāh alone deserves the exclusive submission. (Az-Zumar, 39:2-3)

Then it reiterates the command:

قُلْ إِنِّيٓ أُمِرْتُ أَنْ أَعْبُدَ ٱللَّهَ مُخْلِصًا لَّهُ ٱلدِّينَ ﴿١١﴾

Say, "I have been ordered to worship Allāh, making my submission exclusive to Him. (Az-Zumar, 39:11)

And again it asserts a statement of fact:

قُلِ ٱللَّهَ أَعۡبُدُ مُخۡلِصٗا لَّهُۥ دِينِي ﴿١٤﴾

Say, "It is Allāh whom I worship, making my submission exclusive to Him. (Az-Zumar, 39:14)

Those who believe in Allāh being the sole creator and master of this universe still run the danger of losing the purity of their devotion due to lusts and desires. Attaining and maintaining this purity is a life long struggle.

It helps to realize that of all groups of Muslims, the Companions had the highest level of sincerity. And their unique status is due entirely to it. That is why Allāh announced in the Qur'ān that He was pleased with them, while Allāh does not accept anything which has any taint of insincerity. Learning about their lives and keeping an eye on their examples is thus an effective way of nurturing this sincerity.

Turning Back to Allāh

قُلۡ يَٰعِبَادِيَ ٱلَّذِينَ أَسۡرَفُواْ عَلَىٰٓ أَنفُسِهِمۡ لَا تَقۡنَطُواْ مِن رَّحۡمَةِ ٱللَّهِۚ إِنَّ ٱللَّهَ يَغۡفِرُ ٱلذُّنُوبَ جَمِيعًاۚ إِنَّهُۥ هُوَ ٱلۡغَفُورُ ٱلرَّحِيمُ ﴿٥٣﴾ وَأَنِيبُوٓاْ إِلَىٰ رَبِّكُمۡ وَأَسۡلِمُواْ لَهُۥ مِن قَبۡلِ أَن يَأۡتِيَكُمُ ٱلۡعَذَابُ ثُمَّ لَا تُنصَرُونَ ﴿٥٤﴾

Say: "(Thus speaks Allāh:) 'O my servants who have transgressed against your own selves! Despair not of Allāh's mercy: behold, Allāh forgives all sins. Surely, He is the One who is the Most-Forgiving, the Very-Merciful. Hence, turn towards your Sustainer (alone) and surrender yourselves unto Him before the suffering (of death and resurrection) comes upon you, for then you will not be helped."(Az-Zumar, 39:53-54)

This is such a reassuring message for those who have sinned. By sinning we transgress against our own selves. But the All Merciful Allāh will still turn to us with mercy if we turn to Him in repentance. He is Most-Forgiving; there is no sin He will not forgive if we sincerely seek His forgiveness and take corrective action. The pencil which has been given to us to draw the course of our life's journey does come with a huge eraser. It lasts as long as the pencil itself. There are no signs on the highway of life that prohibit a U-turn. No matter how messed up our lives may have been, we can always correct course. The door to repentance is always open—until the very end of our life. But if we wait too long and the end comes in sight, then repentance will not help.

Admonishment to Pharaoh

يَٰقَوۡمِ لَكُمُ ٱلۡمُلۡكُ ٱلۡيَوۡمَ ظَٰهِرِينَ فِي ٱلۡأَرۡضِ فَمَن يَنصُرُنَا مِنۢ بَأۡسِ
ٱللَّهِ إِن جَآءَنَاۚ قَالَ فِرۡعَوۡنُ مَآ أُرِيكُمۡ إِلَّا مَآ أَرَىٰ وَمَآ أَهۡدِيكُمۡ إِلَّا
سَبِيلَ ٱلرَّشَادِ ٢٩ وَقَالَ ٱلَّذِيٓ ءَامَنَ يَٰقَوۡمِ إِنِّيٓ أَخَافُ عَلَيۡكُم مِّثۡلَ يَوۡمِ
ٱلۡأَحۡزَابِ ٣٠ مِثۡلَ دَأۡبِ قَوۡمِ نُوحٖ وَعَادٖ وَثَمُودَ وَٱلَّذِينَ مِنۢ بَعۡدِهِمۡۚ وَمَا
ٱللَّهُ يُرِيدُ ظُلۡمٗا لِّلۡعِبَادِ ٣١

"O my people, the kingdom is yours today, while you are dominant on the land. But, who is going to help us against Allāh's punishment, if it comes upon us?" Pharaoh said, "I do not give you an opinion unless I myself believe it to be correct, and I do not direct you to anything but to the right way." Thereupon exclaimed he who had attained to faith: "O my people! I fear for you something like a day of the (disbelieving) groups (of the past), like the fate of the people of Nūḥ and ʿĀd and Thamūd and those who were after them—and Allāh does not intend to do any injustice to His servants." (Ghāfir, 40:29-31)

The story of the believer in the court of the Pharaoh is described in some detail in this sūrah. He kept his belief to himself for fear of persecution. However when things started to go out of hand, he had to come out and tell the truth. In the first sentence above he spoke of *we* and *us* so as not to alienate them. Upon Pharaoh's rejection of his passionate appeal, he had to tell them "I fear for *you*."

Moral: The inclusive language should be used whenever possible and the exclusive language when necessary.

Fighting Evil with Good

وَلَا تَسْتَوِى ٱلْحَسَنَةُ وَلَا ٱلسَّيِّئَةُ ۚ ٱدْفَعْ بِٱلَّتِى هِىَ أَحْسَنُ فَإِذَا ٱلَّذِى بَيْنَكَ وَبَيْنَهُۥ عَدَٰوَةٌ كَأَنَّهُۥ وَلِىٌّ حَمِيمٌ ﴿٣٤﴾

Good and evil are not equal. Repel (evil) with what is best, and you will see that the one between whom and you was hatred become as if he were a close friend. (Fuṣṣilat, 41:34)

This teaching will keep the callers to Islam from ever going on ego trips in dealing with the opponents. In his commentary on this Sayyidnā ʿAbdullāh ibn ʿAbbās ﷺ said, "Show patience when someone is venting his anger on you. Show forbearance when someone is rude to you. Forgive when someone hurts you." We should never leave the high moral ground in dealing with adversity and it may even win over the most committed enemies.

Juz Twenty Five

The Purpose behind Economic Scarcity

وَلَوْ بَسَطَ ٱللَّهُ ٱلرِّزْقَ لِعِبَادِهِۦ لَبَغَوْا۟ فِى ٱلْأَرْضِ وَلَـٰكِن يُنَزِّلُ بِقَدَرٍ مَّا يَشَآءُ ۚ
إِنَّهُۥ بِعِبَادِهِۦ خَبِيرٌۢ بَصِيرٌ ﴿٢٧﴾

For if Allāh were to grant (in this world) abundant sustenance to (all of) His servants, they would behave on earth with wanton insolence: but as it is, He bestows (His grace) from on high in due measure, as He wills: for, verily, He is fully aware of (the needs of) His creatures, and sees them all. (Ash-Shūrā 42:27)

Economics is the science that deals with the issue of scarcity. However it cannot see the Divine plan behind this scarcity and therefore leads to the same wanton insolence that is meant to be avoided through it. Scarcity of provisions leads to interdependence and makes the working of the human society possible. It also makes us realize our limits and keeps us from being haughty. The result is that we are thankful for the bounties we receive and patient over wants that go unfulfilled.

But when this understanding is not there, it results in exploitation and oppression. We want to have monopoly over the limited resources and use that monopoly for unfair advantage.

That is why Islamization of Economics, and other social and physical sciences, is so important for the welfare of humanity.

Shūrā = Democracy?

وَٱلَّذِينَ ٱسْتَجَابُوا۟ لِرَبِّهِمْ وَأَقَامُوا۟ ٱلصَّلَوٰةَ وَأَمْرُهُمْ شُورَىٰ بَيْنَهُمْ وَمِمَّا رَزَقْنَٰهُمْ يُنفِقُونَ ﴿٣٨﴾

Those who hearken to their Sustainer, and establish regular Prayer; who (conduct) their affairs by mutual Consultation; who spend out of what We bestow on them for Sustenance; (Ash-Shūrā, 42:38)

This āyah highlights the importance of shūrā or the system of mutual consultation for the running of all collective affairs, whether in the family, in a small group or at the highest levels of the Islamic state. When carried out properly, the system shows that the power of the group is much more than the sum of its members. The group benefits from the best of individual resources, talents and ideas. The process of consultation also brings its members closer together, cementing the group. A hadith promises Allāh's succor to those practicing shūrā.

Sometimes people mention Islamic Shūrā as another name for democracy. This is a dangerous oversimplification and ignores the gulf of difference between their philosophical underpinnings. Democracy is not a system of mutual consultation, but a system of negotiation between divergent interests. Each constituency on this negotiating table seeks to gain at the expense of others and will do whatever it can get away with—from vote rigging and gerrymandering to manufacturing consent through slick propaganda campaigns. The division of the community into political factions is part of the blueprint of democracy, as is the permanent division between the ruling and opposition groups.

All of these are the exact opposite of the spirit and purpose of shūrā, where everyone is working towards the same goals and seeks the greatest benefit for the entire group.

The centrifugal tendencies of democracy require some organizing principle to keep the group together. This was provided by territorial nationalism and the nation-state, which has done much harm to humanity. It is no accident that the rise of democracy and the nation-sate has been simultaneous. Needless to say that Islam stands in total opposition to territorial nationalism. It is worth noting that philosopher and poet Muḥammad Iqbal blasted both of them—nation state as well as democracy—as they were emerging a century ago.

Regarding the nation-state he said:

ان تازہ خداؤں میں بڑا سب سے وطن ہے
جو پیرہن اس کا ہے وہ مذہب کا کفن ہے

The biggest of the newly minted gods is the nation-state.
What it chooses for its cloak is the burial shroud of religion.

Regarding democracy he said:

جمہوریت اک طرز حکومت ہے کہ جس میں
بندوں کو گنا کرتے ہیں تولا نہیں کرتے

Democracy is a system of government, in which
Opinions are counted, not weighed.

And he says this on secularism.

جلال پادشاہی ہو یا جمہوری تماشہ ہو
جدا ہو دیں سیاست سے تو رہ جاتی ہے چنگیزی

Whether it is the majesty of monarchy or the show of democracy—
When religion is removed from politics, what is left is barbarism.

The Perils of Affluence

وَلَوْلَآ أَن يَكُونَ ٱلنَّاسُ أُمَّةً وَٰحِدَةً لَّجَعَلْنَا لِمَن يَكْفُرُ بِٱلرَّحْمَٰنِ
لِبُيُوتِهِمْ سُقُفًا مِّن فِضَّةٍ وَمَعَارِجَ عَلَيْهَا يَظْهَرُونَ ﴿٣٣﴾ وَلِبُيُوتِهِمْ
أَبْوَٰبًا وَسُرُرًا عَلَيْهَا يَتَّكِـُٔونَ ﴿٣٤﴾ وَزُخْرُفًا ۚ وَإِن كُلُّ ذَٰلِكَ لَمَّا
مَتَٰعُ ٱلْحَيَوٰةِ ٱلدُّنْيَا ۚ وَٱلْـَٔاخِرَةُ عِندَ رَبِّكَ لِلْمُتَّقِينَ ﴿٣٥﴾

Were it not that all people would become of a single creed (i.e. disbelief), We would have caused, for those who disbelieve in Raḥmān, roofs of their houses to be made of silver, and the stairs as well, on which they would climb, and doors of their homes, and the coaches on which they would recline, and (would have made some of these things) of gold-ornaments. And all this is nothing but an enjoyment of the worldly life. And the Hereafter, with your Lord, is (destined) for the God-fearing. (Az-Zukhruf 43:33-35)

This is a perspective on the perils of gold and silver that is totally ignored today both by the experts and the laymen. It is a mercy of Allāh that He did not make all of the non-believers extremely rich. Otherwise the road to unbelief would become so slippery that no one would escape sliding down to it.

Juz Twenty Six

Sūrah al-Ḥujurāt

Sūrah al-Ḥujurāt contains essential teachings for our collective life and along with sūrah Noor must be part of the core Qur'ānic syllabus for everyone. Here are just some of the highlights from this sūrah.

News Reports

يَـٰٓأَيُّهَا ٱلَّذِينَ ءَامَنُوٓا۟ إِن جَآءَكُمْ فَاسِقٌۢ بِنَبَإٍ فَتَبَيَّنُوٓا۟ أَن تُصِيبُوا۟ قَوْمًۢا بِجَهَـٰلَةٍ
فَتُصْبِحُوا۟ عَلَىٰ مَا فَعَلْتُمْ نَـٰدِمِينَ ۝٦

O you who believe, if a wicked person comes to you with any news, ascertain the truth, lest you harm people unwittingly. (Al-Ḥujurāt, 49:6)

We are required to check the sources before jumping on a news report. If the source is not trustworthy then we must investigate the report itself before spreading it or acting on it. The āyah says that we should not accept a report from a *fāsiq*. The word can be translated as wicked, ungodly, and iniquitous. This gives us much to think about our practices as media consumers for the description fits most mainstream media reports about Islam and Muslims. We know that most of these reports are tainted, yet continue to treat them as reliable.

It should also stop our practice of publishing reports through emails, social networking, blogs, and other channels without ascertaining the credibility of the resource or authenticity of the report.

The āyah also gives another very important message regarding our media policy. It uses the Arabic word إِن, meaning *in case* to describe the situation that a report comes from a fasiq. It does not say إِذ, meaning *when*. It follows that it should not be a normal practice that our news sources are of the type described; we need to develop our own reliable sources of news and information.

Brotherhood

إِنَّمَا ٱلْمُؤْمِنُونَ إِخْوَةٌ فَأَصْلِحُوا۟ بَيْنَ أَخَوَيْكُمْ ۚ وَٱتَّقُوا۟ ٱللَّهَ لَعَلَّكُمْ تُرْحَمُونَ ﴿١٠﴾

The Believers are but a single Brotherhood: So make peace and reconciliation between your two (contending) brothers; and fear Allāh, that you may receive Mercy. (Al-Ḥujurāt, 49:10)

Yūsuf Ali writes: "The enforcement of the Muslim Brotherhood is the greatest social ideal of Islam. On it was based the Prophet's ﷺ Sermon at his last pilgrimage, and Islam cannot be completely realized until this ideal is achieved."

Mocking and the Standup Comedian

يَٰٓأَيُّهَا ٱلَّذِينَ ءَامَنُوا۟ لَا يَسْخَرْ قَوْمٌ مِّن قَوْمٍ عَسَىٰٓ أَن يَكُونُوا۟ خَيْرًا مِّنْهُمْ وَلَا
نِسَآءٌ مِّن نِّسَآءٍ عَسَىٰٓ أَن يَكُنَّ خَيْرًا مِّنْهُنَّ ۖ وَلَا تَلْمِزُوٓا۟ أَنفُسَكُمْ وَلَا تَنَابَزُوا۟
بِٱلْأَلْقَٰبِ ۖ بِئْسَ ٱلِٱسْمُ ٱلْفُسُوقُ بَعْدَ ٱلْإِيمَٰنِ ۚ وَمَن لَّمْ يَتُبْ فَأُو۟لَٰٓئِكَ هُمُ
ٱلظَّٰلِمُونَ ﴿١١﴾

O you who believe! Let not some men among you laugh at other men: It may be that the (latter) are better than the (former): Nor let some women laugh at other women: It may be that the latter are better than the (former): Nor defame each other, nor call each other by (offensive) nicknames: Ill-seeming is a name connoting wickedness, (to be used of one) after he has believed: And those who do not desist are (indeed) doing wrong. (Al-Ḥujurāt, 49:11)

Laughing at someone implies a sense of superiority. So the act is bad both for the harmony of relationships as well as for the spiritual health of the one making fun of the other.

Today mockery, like many other sins, has been turned into an art form and a serious business. With the invasive culture of entertainment which is spreading like a cancer, it has made inroads in areas that would be unthinkable a generation ago. Today in the West there is hardly a major Islamic conference without entertainment from singers, musicians, and comedians. In that atmosphere many may not realize that the standup comedian is a recent American invention. The term standup comic or standup comedian entered Oxford and Webster's dictionaries in 1966. As usual, radio and television were the main channels responsible for its phenomenal spread. Its predecessors were in Vaudeville and Burlesque, two American institutions of popular entertainment, which followed the Minstrel shows of early

1800s. The Minstrel shows made mockery of black people. So much for the dark history of this craft.

Humor is fine when it is within limits. We see examples of it in the Prophet's ﷺ life. But it was not a routine, everyday occurrence. Imam Ghazali says, "It's not appropriate that it should be invoked by one who wants to indulge in it regularly. Excessiveness in humor and practicing it constantly is prohibited."[1] An Arabic saying goes:

المزاح في الكلام كالملح في الطعام
Humor in conversation is like salt in the food.

A little bit of salt makes it tasty and more palatable. The problem of the comedian is that he wants to produce the entire dinner from salt alone. To be sure he presents himself as a social, cultural or political critic. But it is not that he wants to talk about, say, a social issue and while talking a joke comes to mind so he uses it to drive home his point. Instead he looks for jokes to make people laugh and uses the serious issues only to wrap his jokes in. So he comes with imitation bread, meat, and vegetables but in reality all he has is salt. His stock in trade is salty monologues disparaging others to make the audience laugh. And that is a deadly diet.

The Comedian's problem is in the very nature of his job; he must make people laugh. If nobody laughs at his lines then that will be the end of his career. Under that intense pressure he will do whatever it takes to produce the desired results. This overriding concern can be seen in a famous line from George Carlin, who "helped bring stand-up comedy to the very center of American culture" according to Time magazine.[2] He said, "I think it's the duty of the comedian to

1 Imam Aḥmad bin Qudāmah al-Maqdisi, *Mukhtaṣar Minhāj al-Qāsidīn* (Beirut, Lebanon: Dār al-Kutub al-ʿArabi), 160.

2 Richard Zoglin, "How George Carlin Changed Comedy," *Time*, June

find out where the line is drawn and cross it deliberately."[3] This shows why "Muslim comedian" is an oxymoron. For one can either be intent on crossing the line or intent on not crossing it.

Some of the lines are drawn in the āyah quoted above. Others are in hadith. One hadith says, "Woe be to the person who tells lies to make people laugh."[4] Another hadith warns us against causing insults or injury to others. "It is sufficient evil for a person that he should disdain his Muslim brother."[5]

As a side note, it is significant that prohibition of mockery has been done in a gender specific language; men are prohibited from making fun of other men, women of other women. The question of men making fun of women and women making fun of other men does not arise because such mockery takes place in social settings and Islam does not recognize a mixed gender social setting to begin with.

Suspicions, Spying, Backbiting

يَٰٓأَيُّهَا ٱلَّذِينَ ءَامَنُوا۟ ٱجْتَنِبُوا۟ كَثِيرًا مِّنَ ٱلظَّنِّ إِنَّ بَعْضَ ٱلظَّنِّ إِثْمٌ ۖ وَلَا تَجَسَّسُوا۟
وَلَا يَغْتَب بَّعْضُكُم بَعْضًا ۚ أَيُحِبُّ أَحَدُكُمْ أَن يَأْكُلَ لَحْمَ أَخِيهِ مَيْتًا
فَكَرِهْتُمُوهُ ۚ وَٱتَّقُوا۟ ٱللَّهَ ۚ إِنَّ ٱللَّهَ تَوَّابٌ رَّحِيمٌ ﴿١٢﴾

O you who have attained to faith! Avoid most guesswork (about one another)—for, behold, some of (such) guesswork is (in itself) a sin;

23, 2008, http://content.time.com/time/arts/article/0,8599,1817192,00.html.

3 Paul Farhi, "One Comic, Twice the Laughs," *The Washington Post*, Jun 24, 2008, http://articles.washingtonpost.com/2008-06-24/news/36822690_1_george-carlin-gentle-george-lenny-bruce

4 The grandfather of Bahz ibn Ḥakīm ﷺ in *Sunan Abū Dāwūd*, كتاب الأدب [Chapter: Manners].

5 Abū Hurayrah ﷺ in *Ṣaḥīḥ Muslim*, كتاب البر والصلة والآداب [Chapter: Righteousness, Maintaining Ties of Kinship, and Manners]

and do not spy upon one another, and do not backbite one another. Does one of you like that he eats the flesh of his dead brother? You would abhor it. And fear Allāh. Surely Allāh is Most-Relenting, Very-Merciful. (Al-Ḥujurāt, 49:12)

Suspicions, spying, presumption of guilt, backbiting—these are common ailments in most social settings. In addition to telling us that these are deadly diseases (note the very graphic depiction of the reality of backbiting), this āyah is also telling us that the way to get rid of them is only to remember Allāh and have His fear in our heart.

Tribalism

يَٰٓأَيُّهَا ٱلنَّاسُ إِنَّا خَلَقْنَٰكُم مِّن ذَكَرٍ وَأُنثَىٰ وَجَعَلْنَٰكُمْ شُعُوبًا وَقَبَآئِلَ لِتَعَارَفُوٓا۟ ۚ
إِنَّ أَكْرَمَكُمْ عِندَ ٱللَّهِ أَتْقَىٰكُمْ ۚ إِنَّ ٱللَّهَ عَلِيمٌ خَبِيرٌ ﴿١٣﴾

O mankind, We have created you from a male and a female, and made you into races and tribes, so that you may identify one another. Surely the noblest of you, in Allāh's sight, is the one who is the most God-fearing and righteous of you. Surely Allāh is All-Knowing, All-Aware. (Al-Ḥujurāt, 49:13)

This is the universal declaration that alone can end all tribalism, racism, and nationalism of all Jāhiliyyah—modern and ancient. Unfortunately Muslims whose responsibility it was to invite the entire humanity to this declaration have been at the forefront of violating it. These are very powerful words. But their full power will be realized when the world sees them in practice.

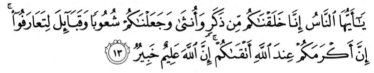

Juz Twenty Seven

Purpose of Our Life

وَمَا خَلَقْتُ ٱلْجِنَّ وَٱلْإِنسَ إِلَّا لِيَعْبُدُونِ ﴿٥٦﴾

I did not create the Jinns and the human beings except for the purpose that they should serve and worship Me. (Adh-Dhāriyāt, 51:56).

'Ibādah, which has been translated as service and worship here, implies total obedience, willing surrender, and dedicated worship. The purpose of our creation and of the freedom of choice given to us is that we choose the path of submission and lead a life of loving service to our Creator. If we do so we'll fulfill the purpose of our creation—which is the very definition of success. Its manifestation will be the everlasting bliss in Paradise. If we fail to do that, our life will have been a failure which will be manifested in the never ending punishment in the Fire.

If we choose other goals in life—goals that are contrary to this goal—then regardless of whether or not we succeed in achieving those goals, our life will have been a failure.

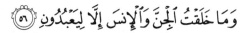

Individual Responsibility

أَلَّا تَزِرُ وَازِرَةٌ وِزْرَ أُخْرَىٰ ﴿٣٨﴾

That no bearer of burdens shall be made to bear another's burden. (An-Najm, 53:38)

As Muhammad Asad writes, this expresses a categorical rejection of the Christian doctrine of the "original sin" with which every human being is allegedly burdened from birth; secondly, it refutes the idea that a person's sins could be "atoned for" by a saint's or a prophet's redemptive sacrifice (as evidenced, for instance, in the Christian doctrine of Jesus' vicarious atonement for mankind's sinfulness, or in the earlier, Persian doctrine of man's vicarious redemption by Mithras).

This also has serious implications in law. No one can be punished for the crimes of another. It thus negates collective punishment as well as guilt by association, principles that are being violated in the new security states now emerging.

Qur'ān is Easy

وَلَقَدْ يَسَّرْنَا ٱلْقُرْءَانَ لِلذِّكْرِ فَهَلْ مِن مُّدَّكِرٍ ﴿١٧﴾

Indeed We have made the Qur'ān easy for seeking advice. Then is there any that will receive admonition?? (Al-Qamar, 54:17)

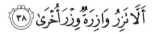

The Arabic word is dhikr, which means remembering, mentioning, reminding, and invocating. This also implies seeking advice. The Qur'ān has been made very easy for all this. Its words are easy to memorize and easy to comprehend and follow. Its simple message solves the riddle of the purpose of creation and our role in this world. Anyone who approaches the Qur'ān with an open mind to seek guidance will be guided by it.

At the same time it is a profound work with an unending store of meanings and fiqhi points within its limited word list. The best of experts may spend a lifetime to unearth them and the store will still not be exhausted. The task of deriving legal rulings is therefore to be entrusted to those who have developed the requisite knowledge and expertise.

Sūrah Ar-Raḥmān

Called the bride of the Qur'ān, this beautiful sūrah has a unique rhythm to it punctuated by the constant refrain, "How many of the bounties of Your Sustainer shall you deny?"

Addressed to both human beings and jinns it describes their creation, reminds them that everything in this universe has a finite lifespan after which it will end and then will be resurrected to face the results of its endeavors—either Hell or Paradise. There is a moving description of both.

The Space for Women

حُورٌ مَّقْصُورَٰتٌ فِي ٱلْخِيَامِ ٧٢

Most beautiful eyed ones (houris) houris, cloistered in cool pavilions. (Ar-Raḥmān, 55:72)

Regarding the maidens of Paradise, it is significant that we do not find them in the public space, where there are eternal young boys as servants. The maidens will be in private pavilions. And they will be happily cloistered in their vast pavilions. *Maqṣūrāt* has also been interpreted to mean restrained as to their glances. Either way they will be leading happy sheltered private lives.

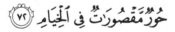

If anyone harbors the suspicion that this arrangement may be uninteresting they may do well to ponder on what the Qur'ān says elsewhere about the Paradise, "Ones who will dwell in them forever. They will have no desire for relocation from there."[1]

Paradise is the ideal state. And if our ideas of the ideal state are at variance from the Qur'ānic description, we need to seriously rethink our ideals.

This Life and That Life

ٱعْلَمُوٓا۟ أَنَّمَا ٱلْحَيَوٰةُ ٱلدُّنْيَا لَعِبٌ وَلَهْوٌ وَزِينَةٌ وَتَفَاخُرٌۢ بَيْنَكُمْ وَتَكَاثُرٌ
فِى ٱلْأَمْوَٰلِ وَٱلْأَوْلَٰدِ ۖ كَمَثَلِ غَيْثٍ أَعْجَبَ ٱلْكُفَّارَ نَبَاتُهُۥ ثُمَّ يَهِيجُ فَتَرَىٰهُ
مُصْفَرًّا ثُمَّ يَكُونُ حُطَٰمًا ۖ وَفِى ٱلْءَاخِرَةِ عَذَابٌ شَدِيدٌ وَمَغْفِرَةٌ مِّنَ ٱللَّهِ
وَرِضْوَٰنٌ ۚ وَمَا ٱلْحَيَوٰةُ ٱلدُّنْيَآ إِلَّا مَتَٰعُ ٱلْغُرُورِ ﴿٢٠﴾

Know (O men) that the life of this world is but a play and a diversion, and pageantry, and (the cause of) your boastful vying with one another, and (of your) greed for more and more riches and children. Its parable is that of (life-giving) rain: the herbage which it causes to grow delights the tillers of the soil; but then it withers, and you can see it turn yellow; and in the end it crumbles into dust. But (the abiding truth of man's condition will become fully apparent) in the life to come: (either) suffering severe, or God's forgiveness and His goodly acceptance: for the life of this world is nothing but an enjoyment of self-delusion. (Al-Ḥadīd, 57:20)

This is a description of the life lived in this world without concern for the life to come. Like the vegetation that brings delightful greenery and then withers and crumbles, this life goes through its cycles and no stage in this cycle is permanent, no matter how badly we may wish it to be. Permanence

1 *Al-Qur'ān*, al-Kahf 18:108.

belongs to the life to come. And wisdom is in not letting the fleeting pleasures distract us from the permanent ones.

One result of developing the correct outlook here will be a graceful life that will not be unduly impacted by the highs and lows of life. As the following āyah says: "so that you may neither grieve on what has escaped you, nor over-exult on what He has given to you."[2]

2 *Al-Qur'ān*, al-Hadīd 57:23.

Juz Twenty Eight

The Peril of Humanism

وَلَا تَكُونُوا كَالَّذِينَ نَسُوا اللَّهَ فَأَنسَاهُمْ أَنفُسَهُمْ ۚ أُولَٰئِكَ هُمُ الْفَاسِقُونَ ﴿١٩﴾

Do not be like those who forgot Allāh, so He made them forget their own souls. It is they who are truly depraved. (Al-Ḥashr, 59:19)

Why does the Qur'ān emphasize remembrance of Allāh so much? It is for our own good. Allāh is in no need of our worship or our remembrance. As a hadith points out if the entire body of humans and jinns were to engage in such an intensive worship and remembrance of Allāh that they did nothing else, it would not add an iota to the majesty and power of Allāh. If all of them became totally disobedient, that would not take away even an iota from it.

But we need it. Our lives have no meaning and our endeavors have no purpose when we are disconnected from our Creator and Master. Being oblivious of Allāh in fact amounts to being oblivious of what is good and bad for our own souls. This is what humanism has done as an ideology. By making the human being instead of God as the center of its universe, it has caused the humanity to sink into a life of utter depravity.

The study of "humanities" thus has a problem with its very foundations. Unless that foundation is corrected by going back to a God-centered world, this education will be spreading ignorance instead of knowledge.

Judging Others

Muslim Women Marrying Non-Muslim Men

يَٰٓأَيُّهَا ٱلَّذِينَ ءَامَنُوٓاْ إِذَا جَآءَكُمُ ٱلْمُؤْمِنَٰتُ مُهَٰجِرَٰتٍ فَٱمْتَحِنُوهُنَّ ۖ ٱللَّهُ أَعْلَمُ
بِإِيمَٰنِهِنَّ ۖ فَإِنْ عَلِمْتُمُوهُنَّ مُؤْمِنَٰتٍ فَلَا تَرْجِعُوهُنَّ إِلَى ٱلْكُفَّارِ ۖ لَا هُنَّ حِلٌّ لَّهُمْ وَلَا
هُمْ يَحِلُّونَ لَهُنَّ

O You who have attained to faith! Whenever believing women come unto you, forsaking the domain of evil, examine them, (although only) Allāh is fully aware of their faith; and if you have thus ascertained that they are believers, do not send them back to the deniers of the truth, (since) they are not (any longer) lawful to their erstwhile husbands, and these are not (any longer) lawful to them. (Al-Mumtaḥinah, 60:10)

This āyah is categorical that Muslim women cannot be married to non-Muslim men.

By asking the community to decide the issue of faith of a claimant through examination the āyah also dissipates a common confusion about the issue of judging what is in people's hearts. Only Allāh knows what is truly in people's hearts as the āyah reiterates. Yet it asks us to deal with these women based on the results of our own examination.

Many a time we do need to make a judgment about people's intentions and faith in order to deal with them. For marriages or business dealings, we need to judge whether the other person is sincere. Courts need to judge the intentions of the accused to decide the gravity of his actions. Whether a person has true faith or not is known with certainty by Allāh alone. But since we need the information to decide our dealings with them, we judge based on apparent evidence. In doing so we fully realize that in the Hereafter everyone will be judged by Allāh and we cannot make any declarations with certainty as to what that judgment will be.

A well-known saying of Sayyidnā ʿUmar ibn al-Khaṭṭāb رضي الله عنه makes it clear. "We decide based on apparent evidence and Allāh knows the secrets in people's hearts."

Prophet Muḥammad ﷺ in the Bible

وَإِذْ قَالَ عِيسَى ٱبْنُ مَرْيَمَ يَٰبَنِىٓ إِسْرَٰٓءِيلَ إِنِّى رَسُولُ ٱللَّهِ إِلَيْكُم مُّصَدِّقًا لِّمَا بَيْنَ يَدَىَّ
مِنَ ٱلتَّوْرَىٰةِ وَمُبَشِّرًۢا بِرَسُولٍ يَأْتِى مِنۢ بَعْدِى ٱسْمُهُۥٓ أَحْمَدُ

And (this happened, too,) when Jesus, the son of Mary, said: "O children of Israel! Behold, I am an apostle of Allāh unto you, (sent) to confirm the truth of whatever there still remains of the Torah, and to give (you) the glad tiding of an apostle who shall come after me, whose name shall be Ahmad." (Aṣ-Ṣaff, 61:6)

Muhammad Asad writes: "This prediction is supported by several references in the Gospel of St. John to the Parklûtos (usually rendered as "Comforter") who was to come after Jesus. This designation is almost certainly a corruption of Peraklytos ("the Much-Praised"), an exact Greek translation of the Aramaic term or name Mawhamana. (It is to be borne in mind that Aramaic was the language used in Palestine at the time of, and for some centuries after, Jesus, and was thus undoubtedly the language in which the original—now lost—texts of the Gospels were composed.) In view of the phonetic closeness of Peraklytos and Paraklûtos it is easy to understand how the translator—or, more probably, a later scribe—confused these two expressions. It is significant that both the Aramaic Mawhamana and the Greek Peraklytos have the same meaning as the two names of the Last Prophet, Muḥammad and Aḥmad, both of which are derived from the verb *ḥamida* ("he praised") and the noun *ḥamd* ("praise")."

An even more unequivocal prediction of the advent of the Prophet Muḥammad ﷺ—mentioned by name, in its Arabic form—is in Gospel of St. Barnabas, which was accepted as authentic and was read in the churches until the year 496 of the Christian era, when it was banned as "heretical" by a decree of Pope Gelasius.

Useless Knowledge

مَثَلُ ٱلَّذِينَ حُمِّلُوا۟ ٱلتَّوْرَىٰةَ ثُمَّ لَمْ يَحْمِلُوهَا كَمَثَلِ ٱلْحِمَارِ يَحْمِلُ أَسْفَارًۢا ۚ بِئْسَ مَثَلُ ٱلْقَوْمِ ٱلَّذِينَ كَذَّبُوا۟ بِـَٔايَـٰتِ ٱللَّهِ ۚ وَٱللَّهُ لَا يَهْدِى ٱلْقَوْمَ ٱلظَّـٰلِمِينَ ﴿٥﴾

The parable of those who were graced with the burden of the Torah, and thereafter failed to bear it, is that of an ass that carries a load of books (but cannot benefit from them). Calamitous is the parable of people who are bent on giving the lie to Allāh's messages—for Allāh does not bestow His guidance upon such evildoing folk! (Al-Jumuʿah, 62:5)

Knowledge that is not accompanied by true understanding and practice is as useful for the holder of that knowledge as the books are for the donkey carrying them.

Deceptive Appearances

وَإِذَا رَأَيْتَهُمْ تُعْجِبُكَ أَجْسَامُهُمْ ۖ وَإِن يَقُولُوا تَسْمَعْ لِقَوْلِهِمْ ۖ كَأَنَّهُمْ خُشُبٌ مُّسَنَّدَةٌ

And if you see them, their physiques would attract you, and if they speak, you would (like to) listen to their speech (because of their eloquence). (Yet, being devoid of substance,) it is as if they were propped up beams of timber. (Al-Munāfiqūn, 63:4)

This is a description of the hypocrites. In the media age one wonders how many are the sought-after celebrities with carefully groomed appearances and telegenic personalities who have perfected the art of slick talks who precisely fit the description. They are wooden props on a stage, not real human beings.

This should always remind us not to confuse eloquence with scholarship or video images with reality.

Way Out of Hardships

وَمَن يَتَّقِ ٱللَّهَ يَجْعَل لَّهُۥ مَخْرَجًا ﴿٢﴾ وَيَرْزُقْهُ مِنْ حَيْثُ لَا يَحْتَسِبُ ۚ وَمَن يَتَوَكَّلْ عَلَى ٱللَّهِ فَهُوَ حَسْبُهُۥٓ ۚ إِنَّ ٱللَّهَ بَٰلِغُ أَمْرِهِۦ ۚ قَدْ جَعَلَ ٱللَّهُ لِكُلِّ شَىْءٍ قَدْرًا ﴿٣﴾

Whoever fears Allāh, He brings forth a way out for him, and provides him (with what he needs) from where he does not even imagine. And whoever places his trust in Allāh, He is sufficient for him. Surely Allāh is to accomplish His purpose. Allāh has set a measure for every thing. (Aṭ-Ṭalāq, 65:2-3)

When we are in a difficulty and all doors out of it seem to be closed, reciting this āyah repeatedly will bring comfort to our heart as well as ease from unexpected sources.

Juz Twenty Nine

Life and Death

تَبَـٰرَكَ ٱلَّذِى بِيَدِهِ ٱلْمُلْكُ وَهُوَ عَلَىٰ كُلِّ شَىْءٍ قَدِيرٌ ﴿١﴾ ٱلَّذِى خَلَقَ ٱلْمَوْتَ
وَٱلْحَيَوٰةَ لِيَبْلُوَكُمْ أَيُّكُمْ أَحْسَنُ عَمَلًا ۚ وَهُوَ ٱلْعَزِيزُ ٱلْغَفُورُ ﴿٢﴾

Glorious is the One in whose hand is the Kingdom (of the whole universe), and He is powerful over everything, the One who created death and life, so that He may test you as to which of you is better in his deeds. And He is the All-Mighty, the Most-Forgiving. (Al-Mulk, 67:1-2)

This is the answer to the basic questions of life and death. This entire universe is in the hands of Allāh, Who has full control over its running. He created the system of life and death, so nobody can escape it. Those destined to be born will be born. And everyone who is born will die one day. Then people will be judged and rewarded or punished based on the goodness of their deeds or lack thereof. It follows that for those who hold this worldview it is incumbent that they find out what the good deeds are so they can perform them and what the bad deeds are so they can avoid them.

Listening- Reasoning

وَقَالُوا۟ لَوْ كُنَّا نَسْمَعُ أَوْ نَعْقِلُ مَا كُنَّا فِىٓ أَصْحَـٰبِ ٱلسَّعِيرِ ﴿١٠﴾

And they will add: "Had we but listened (to those warnings), or (at least) used our own reason, we would not (now) be among those who are destined for the blazing flame!" (Al-Mulk, 67:10)

This is the statement of the people judged to go to Hell. When asked whether anybody had warned them about this dreadful result they will readily admit that the warners had come and they had flatly rejected them. In rejecting the Messengers today they may be waxing eloquent about how the use of their sense perceptions and reason dictates this rejection. When they come face to face with Hell, they will suddenly realize that they had not really used their faculties of hearing and reasoning at all. On that day they will be volunteering this admission on their own. This is what the Qur'ān says elsewhere about the rejecters of faith:

وَلَقَدْ ذَرَأْنَا لِجَهَنَّمَ كَثِيرًا مِّنَ ٱلْجِنِّ وَٱلْإِنسِ ۖ لَهُمْ قُلُوبٌ لَّا يَفْقَهُونَ بِهَا وَلَهُمْ أَعْيُنٌ لَّا يُبْصِرُونَ بِهَا وَلَهُمْ ءَاذَانٌ لَّا يَسْمَعُونَ بِهَآ ۚ أُو۟لَـٰٓئِكَ كَٱلْأَنْعَـٰمِ بَلْ هُمْ أَضَلُّ ۚ أُو۟لَـٰٓئِكَ هُمُ ٱلْغَـٰفِلُونَ ﴿١٧٩﴾

Many are the Jinns and men We have made for Hell: They have hearts wherewith they understand not, eyes wherewith they see not, and ears wherewith they hear not. They are like cattle—nay more misguided: for they are heedless (of warning). (Al-Aʿrāf 7:179)

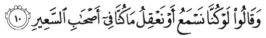

The tools of our sense perception and reasoning are not sufficient to find out the Truth about the deeper issues of life and death on our own. But they are sufficient to confirm the veracity of the Messengers who have been sent by Allāh to answer these questions. Those who reject the messengers have failed to use these tools properly.

Human Weakness and its Treatment

إِنَّ ٱلْإِنسَٰنَ خُلِقَ هَلُوعًا ﴿١٩﴾ إِذَا مَسَّهُ ٱلشَّرُّ جَزُوعًا ﴿٢٠﴾ وَإِذَا مَسَّهُ ٱلْخَيْرُ
مَنُوعًا ﴿٢١﴾ إِلَّا ٱلْمُصَلِّينَ ﴿٢٢﴾ ٱلَّذِينَ هُمْ عَلَىٰ صَلَاتِهِمْ دَآئِمُونَ ﴿٢٣﴾

Surely man was created fretful, when evil visits him, impatient, when good visits him, grudging. Not so, however, those who consciously turn towards Allāh in ṣalāh (and) who incessantly persevere in their ṣalāh (Al-Maʿārij, 70:19-23)

This is a general human weakness, born out of myopia. This will be reduced to the extent a person can keep his eyes on the long term. The longest term is that which encompasses the Hereafter. And therefore it is the practicing believers alone who escape this. Ṣalāh (prayer) has a central role in building a strong character and helping us overcome this weakness and therefore praying regularly is the first attribute mentioned here.

Juz Thirty

Vain Speech

لَّا يَسْمَعُونَ فِيهَا لَغْوًا وَلَا كِذَّابًا ﴿٣٥﴾

No vanity shall they hear therein, nor Untruth. (An-Naba', 78:35)

For most people the idea of having a nice time in a luxurious garden setting invariably involves gossiping with friends. And gossip, in order to be fun, tends to consist of vain conversation and, embellishments, even lies. By promising the total absence of such speech in Paradise, the Qur'ān is reforming our idea of fun. Paradise is the ideal place. Every possible means of joy will be there. If something will not be there, that is sufficient evidence that that thing is not enjoyable or desirable, regardless of its appearance.

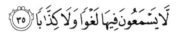

Got it Made?

فَأَمَّا ٱلْإِنسَٰنُ إِذَا مَا ٱبْتَلَىٰهُ رَبُّهُۥ فَأَكْرَمَهُۥ وَنَعَّمَهُۥ فَيَقُولُ رَبِّىٓ أَكْرَمَنِ ﴿١٥﴾

As for man, when his Sustainer tries him, giving him honor and bounties, he says (puffed up), "My Sustainer has honored me." (Al-Fajr, 89:15)

This is the description of a shallow person. Due to his very narrow perspective, he sees the achievements in this life as rewards instead of tests. The person in this āyah still remembers God. Many people today simply say, "I got it made." The easily puffed up person also is easily turned to despair when the going goes tough as the next āyah says.

وَأَمَّآ إِذَا مَا ٱبْتَلَىٰهُ فَقَدَرَ عَلَيْهِ رِزْقَهُۥ فَيَقُولُ رَبِّىٓ أَهَٰنَنِ ﴿١٦﴾

But when He tries him, and thus straitens his provision for him, he says (in despair), "My Sustainer has humiliated me!" (Al-Fajr, 89:16)

Immediately after describing these habits, the Qur'ān adds an emphatic *kallā*. Nay. Not at all. This is not so. If you accumulated a lot of wealth, position, and prestige in this world, this does not necessarily mean Allāh is pleased with you. If you have none of these, it does not necessarily mean that Allāh is angry with you. It is the beginning of wisdom that we stop confusing the test with the test results.

Perspective on Iqra

ٱقْرَأْ بِٱسْمِ رَبِّكَ ٱلَّذِى خَلَقَ ﴿١﴾

Read in the name of your Sustainer, who has created. (Al-'Alaq, 96:1).

This is the very first āyah that started the revelations that lasted for twenty three years. It is a very famous āyah. It is also a greatly misused āyah. We frequently hear that the first Qur'ānic command was to read. With that we justify all sorts of activities that go on in the name of education.

The irony is that we stop reading immediately after the word "read." For the very first command was not simply "Read." It was "Read in the name of your Lord." And there is a world of difference between the two.

To understand the difference, we can look more closely at the revelations. The very first revelation consisted of five āyahs. It began with this āyah and ended with, "He taught man what he did not know."[1] The command was not to read anything and everything, but to read with a purpose and a proper perspective. Allāh is the source of true knowledge. And the command is to acquire that knowledge.

The remaining āyahs of this sūrah were revealed sometime later. And here is how the sūrah that began with the word Iqra ended: "bow down in sajdah, and come close to Me." [2]This is the logical result of reading done in the name of Allāh. It impels the person to prostrate himself before his Creator and thus brings him closer to Him. We can judge whether we are reading as commanded by seeing if it is producing the result as mentioned in the command.

Further, the entire sequence of revelations ended twenty-three years later. And it is also very instructive to see how that happened. The very last āyah to be revealed said: And be conscious of the Day on which you shall be brought back unto Allāh, whereupon every human being shall be repaid in full for what he has earned, and none shall be wronged.[3]

---

1 *Al-Qur'ān*, al-ʿAlaq 96:5.

2 *Al-Qur'ān*, al-ʿAlaq 96:19.

3 *Al-Qur'ān*, al-Baqarah 2:281.

This is the ultimate result of reading in the name of Allāh. The command to read was clearly leading in this direction, making us lead Hereafter-conscious lives. If our reading is not doing the same then we are not really following the command. It is a great travesty that our current education systems are promoted and justified by invoking this āyah, although they are not at all informed by it.

Appendix

Qur'ān: Witness the Miracle

Night after night in Ramadan, the believers witness a unique spectacle at masjids around the world. They stand in special Tarāwīḥ prayers in which the prayer leader will recite the entire Qur'ān from memory. Those who have accomplished this extraordinary feat of memorizing all of the 6,236 verses are not a handful of devotees but there are hundreds of thousands of them. Most, just like most Muslims in the world today, do not speak Arabic. Yet they have painstakingly learned to pronounce each and every word of the Qur'ān correctly. The phenomenon is not a result of some religious resurgence that would pass. From the very first day that the Qur'ān was revealed, it was memorized. And the number of those who have memorized it has been increasing ever since. Memorization of the Qur'ān has been going on all through the centuries, all over the globe wherever Muslims are.

There are other religions that claim to possess the Word of God. There is none that can show a book that has commanded anything even remotely comparable to this level of devotion. The Qur'ān is the most read and the only completely memorized book in the whole world. It is also the most studied book in the world. It has stimulated development of entire disciplines of knowledge dealing with its reading, writing, and interpretation.

Miraculous as it is, this is not the only unique aspect of the Qur'ān.

The Qur'ān was the first book in the Arabic language. Yet fourteen centuries later, its language is as alive as it was when it was revealed. And there is no other example when the very first book in a language became any masterpiece let alone the eternal masterpiece that the Qur'ān is. Further, there is no other language of the world that has withstood the passage of fourteen centuries. Over the centuries, rivers change courses, civilizations rise and fall, and languages become extinct and new ones develop. Consider the expression "faeder ure on heofonum" from Lord's Prayer in Matthew 6 from a Bible of 900 CE. We are told it means "our father in heaven." It also means that any writing from that time cannot be read by an English speaker today. But any Arabic speaker can open the Qur'ān today and understand its message. As did all the people in the intervening centuries!

Prominent scholar Dr. Hamidullah tells of an effort in Germany by the Christian scholars to gather all the Greek manuscripts of Bible as the original Bible in Aramaic is extinct. They gathered all manuscripts in the world and after examining them reported: "Some two hundred thousand contradictory narrations have been found . . . of these one-eighth are of an important nature." When the report was published, some people established an Institute for Qur'ānic Research in Munich with the goal of examining the Qur'ān the same way. A gigantic research project was started that continued for three generations. By 1933, 43,000 photocopies of Qur'ānic manuscripts had been collected. A report published shortly before World War II showed the results of the examination of these manuscripts. While some minor mistakes of calligraphy were found, not a single discrepancy in the text had been discovered!

This Book is meant to command and guide humanity until the end of time. That the passage of fourteen centuries has not made the slightest dent in its language or textual integrity or literary beauty is just one evidence of that unique role; its contents have also been unassailable by the passage of time. It makes statements of scientific facts that science would discover centuries later but none that science could ever refute. It tells about ancient history, like the civilization of the ʿĀd people in the Empty Quarter of the Arabian desert that no other historical sources, then or since, contain any information about. Yet, its veracity has only recently been verified by scientific discoveries. Above all, it provides a system of beliefs and a code of conduct for life that is as relevant, illuminating, and true today, as it was fourteen centuries earlier and during all the centuries in between.

The believers know that this Book had to be above space and time because this is the Word of the Creator of space and time. And He has promised that it will always be above space and time. But those who are looking from the outside and are just curious may consider these additional facts:

Prophet Muḥammad ﷺ did not go to any school, study from any teacher, or even learn how to read and write. He even had no interest in poetry, which was one of the most prized disciplines of his time. Yet suddenly at age forty, he began to recite this marvelous revelation.

The style of the Qur'ān is very distinct from the words of the Prophet ﷺ himself, which also have been preserved in Hadith collections. His own sayings are embodiments of eloquence, but they have a different style. Moreover, they clearly are the words of a human being. Although never deviating from the truth, they do show human emotions and the effects of the circumstances in which they were said. The Qur'ān, on the other hand, never shows the slightest trace of these effects. It always speaks from above.

It was revealed over a twenty-three year period and covers a very wide range of subjects yet it shows neither a gradual development of style nor any self-contradictions in the voluminous text.

The twenty-three years of Prophetic life was not a period spent in isolation. He did not retire to a cave to produce this miraculous work. The Prophet ﷺ did spend long periods of time in quiet meditation in Cave Hirā' before becoming a Prophet. But after Prophethood was conferred upon him, his life was one of constant struggle with the pagans, and later the Jews, of Arabia who spared no effort to stop and persecute him. It was during this period of persecution, wars, campaigns, and solving problems associated with the bringing about of the greatest civilizational revolution of all times—an extremely busy and challenging period—that the Qur'ānic Revelation was also received and compiled.

The Prophet ﷺ himself was most deeply moved by the Book. He used to stand for hours in solitary midnight prayers reciting from the Book until his feet would get swollen. How preposterous that one should attempt to attribute the Book to him. Has there ever been another example of somebody getting so moved by his own words?

This is not meant to be an exhaustive list of all the evidence that proves the Qur'ān to be the Word of God. Scholars have written books expounding the miracle of miracles that the Qur'ān is. But even this small sampler may propel an inquiring mind to go and read the Book himself.

To read this Book with an open mind is to believe in it. Those who sincerely seek guidance will find their questions answered, their confusions removed, and their problems solved in its pages. From the beginning until the end, every word in the Qur'ān tells the reader that it is the Word of Allāh. And those who ignore it do so at their own peril.

وَإِن كُنتُمْ فِي رَيْبٍ مِّمَّا نَزَّلْنَا عَلَىٰ عَبْدِنَا فَأْتُوا۟ بِسُورَةٍ مِّن مِّثْلِهِۦ
وَٱدْعُوا۟ شُهَدَآءَكُم مِّن دُونِ ٱللَّهِ إِن كُنتُمْ صَٰدِقِينَ ﴿٢٣﴾ فَإِن لَّمْ
تَفْعَلُوا۟ وَلَن تَفْعَلُوا۟ فَٱتَّقُوا۟ ٱلنَّارَ ٱلَّتِي وَقُودُهَا ٱلنَّاسُ وَٱلْحِجَارَةُ أُعِدَّتْ
لِلْكَٰفِرِينَ ﴿٢٤﴾

And if you are in doubt as to what We have revealed to Our servant, then produce a surah (chapter) like thereof; and call your witnesses or helpers (if there are any) besides Allāh, if your (doubts) are true. But if you cannot—and of a surety you cannot—then fear the Fire whose fuel is men and stones, which is prepared for those who reject Faith. (Al-Baqarah, 2:23-24)

[This article was originally published in the author's first book *First Things First* (2004).]

Glossary

āyah: (plural ayāt) is the basic unit of the Qur'ān. It means sign or evidence. It is generally translated as verse. But it is best to leave the terms (like manzil, surah, and juz or para) associated with the Qur'ān un-translated.

Ḥadīth: The sayings and the traditions of Prophet Muḥammad ﷺ or his actions, or the words or actions of others that he witnessed and tacitly approved.

ḥijāb: The external dress for women used to hide their attractiveness from non-maḥram men.

ḥayā': Sense of shame and modesty. The inner force that keeps us from committing inappropriate actions. A key Islāmic moral value.

Ibrāhīm: Abraham

īmān: Faith

ʿĪsā: Jesus.

isrāf: Extravagance.

Jāhiliyyah: Ignorance. In Islāmic history it refers to the pre-Islāmic era that existed in Arabia after the teachings of Prophet Ibrāhīm عليه السلام and Ismāʿīl عليه السلام had been lost resulting in widespread immorality, oppression, and evil.

Mūsā: Moses.

mushrikīn: Polytheists, people who commit shirk.

Nūh: Noah.

Qur'ān: The Last and Final Book that Allāh revealed for mankind. It was revealed over a period of twenty-three years through Angel Jibrīl (Gabriel) on to Prophet Muḥammad ﷺ. Note: The Qur'ān is in Arabic. Although it has been translated into nearly every language of the world, those translations cannot be called the Qur'ān. So phrases like the English Qur'ān are meaningless.

ṣalāh: The prescribed act of worship in Islām, which includes the acts of standing, kneeling, and prostrating before Allāh.

sayyidinā: Literally, our master. A term of reverence used to refer to the pious predecessors, especially the prophets and the Ṣaḥābah.

shirk: Polytheism, associating partners with Allāh.

tabdhīr: Spending money in unecessary pursuits.

taqwā: Consciousness of Allāh. Fear of displeasing Allāh by committing acts He prohibited or by failing to do what He commanded.

tawḥīd: The doctrine of the "Oneness of God." This is a central tenet of Islām, upon which all other beliefs and doctrines are based.

Yūsuf: Joseph.

Index

A

B

C

D

E

F

G

H

I

J

K

L

M

U

V

W

Y

Z

Also from Open Mind Press

the Accepted Whispers
"Munājāt-e-Maqbūl"

Compiled by Mawlānā Ashraf ʿAlī Thānawī
Translation and commentary by Khalid Baig

A collection of over 200 duʿā's from the Qur'ān and Ḥadīth for daily reading.

176 pp. 5.5 x 8.5 in. Paperback
Also available in pocket size (arabic and english translation)

Duʿā' (supplication) is the essence of worship. It is the weapon of the believer. With it we can never fail; without it we can never succeed. It is a whispering conversation with Allāh, the most uplifting, liberating, empowering, and transforming conversation one can ever have.

This book contains more than 200 duʿā's from the Qur'ān and Ḥadīth in Arabic for daily reading, along with their transliteration, translation, and commentary in English. The commentary explains historic background, meanings, merits, and special significance of the duʿā' in question.

"Khalid Baig's writing is indeed inspiring. *The Accepted Whispers* is no exception. It is a source of immense solace; an orchard lush with spiritual harmony. This is essential reading for the young and the old.

— Moulana Ebrahim Bham
Council of Muslim Theologians (Jamiatul 'Ulama), South Africa"

To order, contact:

Slippery Stone: An Inquiry Into Islam's Stance on Music

BY KHALID BAIG

This book demystifies the issue of music in Islam by going to original source books in Arabic, many of them brought to light for the first time in the English language. It traces the attitudes of the Muslim society about music throughout its history and quotes extensively from the deliberations of the Qur'ān and Ḥadīth scholars, Sufi masters, and jurists from all schools of Islāmic Law, both Sunnī and Shīʿah.

384 PP. 6 X 9 IN. PAPERBACK

Khalid Baig has done a marvelous job of bringing together every traditional, shar'ee, and historic evidence regarding the status of music in Islam.

— IMAM TAHIR ANWAR

IMAM AND DIRECTOR, SOUTH BAY ISLAMIC ASSOCIATION, CALIFORNIA, USA

This work is sure to become a standard reference in its field for many years to come.

— SHAYKH YASIR QADHI

DEAN OF ACADEMIC AFFAIRS, ALMAGHRIB INSTITUTE, USA

Contemporary, convincing, comprehensive . . . this book is a must read for all who wish to learn about this subject.

— MUFTI ZUBAIR BAYAT

DARUL IHSAN RESEARCH AND EDUCATION CENTRE

Simply outstanding. ...a kind of book that is seldom available on a contemporary issue.

— DR. MUZAFFAR IQBAL

PRESIDENT, CENTER FOR THE STUDY OF ISLAM AND SCIENCE, CANADA

The author deserves credit for bringing into relief in a highly balanced way the Islamic position on music . . . [He] is to be complimented for having addressed a complex issue so astutely and in the truly Islamic perspective

— MUSLIM WORLD BOOK REVIEW